The Legacy of Absence

RESOLVING THE WOUNDS

FROM UNINVOLVED FATHERS IN

INDIVIDUALS, FAMILIES, AND SOCIETY

TIM OLSON

TIM OLSON LIFE COACH, LLC

Most names shared in this volume have been changed to protect identities. Some stories and details have been condensed for brevity's sake with much care taken to preserve original facts, actions and intentions. Where I've gotten details and timelines out of sorts, it was purely unintentional. This book is not intended to provide therapy, counseling, clinical advice or treatment or to take the place of the same as provided therapy, counseling, clinical advice or treatment or to take the place of the same as provided from your personal medical and mental health providers. Readers are advised to consult their own qualified healthcare professional regarding mental health or medical issues. Neither the publisher nor the author take any responsibility for any possible consequences from any treatment, action, or application of information in this book to the reader.

The Legacy of Absence: Resolving the Wounds from Uninvolved Fathers In Individuals, Families, and Society / Tim Olson

ISBN: 978-1-54398-861-1 (sc)
ISBN: 978-1-54398-862-8 (e)

Library of Congress Control Number: 2019916000

Cover Design: BookBaby
Cover Image: BookBaby
Copy/Line Editor: Brannan Sirratt
Content editor: Kimberly Kessler
Graphic Artist: Mike Stenberg

Printed in the United States of America

This book is dedicated to all the men and women still aching to hear their father say, "I love you."

Table of Contents

Introduction

The Ultimate Problem

There is clear evidence that all the problems in society can be traced back to fathers being uninvolved in the lives of their children. I've seen firsthand the painful effects this has on the lives of individuals, from all walks of life. Undoubtedly, you have, too, although you may not have realized that fathers are the true culprit.

Rest assured it will be clear as you read that these effects appear at every level of society. In family life, business, schools, governments, and prisons; in married-with-children and single-parent families; in men and women of all ages and races. Living fatherless is a human problem, one now at pandemic proportions.

We have the data. We know the scope of the problem. And yet, where are the solutions? The answer to father uninvolvement is simple: engage in active and intentional father presence.

But not all answers have simple solutions.

There are multiple obstacles that stand in the way of real solutions. These obstacles are generational, cultural, pervasive, and fundamentally relational. In order to overcome them, we must *recognize* our unique individual and cultural struggles and *respond* with equally unique solutions.

To create the change we need, we must support and advocate father involvement at the highest levels of society—with action and authority.

Without this level of invested intent, the cycle won't stop, the wounds of uninvolvement won't heal.

And oh, how we need our wounds to heal.

One point for clarity: While overlapping in many ways, the roles of the father and mother are different. Not better or worse, simply different. Both are significant and powerful. In the analysis that follows, we will discuss the dynamics of fathers who are involved or not —physically, mentally, and emotionally. The various roles of the mother are also introduced for the purpose of further understanding the role of the father but are not examined outside of that context.

The purpose is not to avoid, diminish, or exclude the mother, but to focus on the father and father wound. To attempt to address both in their entirety would go beyond the scope of intention and muddle the critical message the world needs about fathers. Certainly, the mother wound is another fascinating topic that needs to be better understood and addressed as well, but in a separate book.

A second point for clarity: At times you will see statistics and examples cited where the traditional family model is shown to be a highly effective model for active father presence. And it is! But it's not the only model.

The path to an involved fatherhood is not a one-size fits all solution, especially in today's culture. While the need for a positive father presence exists in every individual, achieving this connection is possible in *any* family, regardless of the physical and emotional availability of the biological father.

This book endeavors to show you how.

And a third, essential point: Recognize that supporting and involving fathers does *not* mean overturning other social progress. This is not a call for us to wind back the equality clock. In fact, it's just the opposite. Owning our reality that father uninvolvement is the root of our problems is the first step to simplifying our path and paving the way to our solution: involved father presence.

Involved father presence has the potential to be a conduit for health and progress in all areas of society. The benefits that children with active father presence receive are overwhelming, countering father absence to such a degree that the effects extend from individuals to families to communities to nations—for generations to come.

Uninvolved fathering may be destroying our world, but that simply means active father presence can save it.

In this book we will first look at **The Truth about Uninvolved Fathers** by defining the four modes of fathering and demonstrating what each looks like in action, as well as the real-world consequences, both positive and negative, for individuals, families, and society.

We will explore **The Cycle of Uninvolvement**, including its triggers and root causes that allow it to spread from the individual to families, communities, businesses, political landscapes, and societal norms at large.

Then we will see that power to change our world for the better is possible with **The Cure for Uninvolvement.** When we actively employ father presence, we *can* break the cycle. And when we do that at every level of society—from lawmakers to school administration, community resources, family business, marriages, parent child relationships, and finally within individuals themselves—we can positively affect our present-day lives and the generations to come.

Part I

The Truth about Uninvolved Fathers

Chapter 1

The Power of a Father

"The term 'Father' is the consummate masculine word. It is applied masculinity at its best."

—STU WEBER, AUTHOR

"What we do in this life echoes in eternity."

—MAXIMUS

Every moment of every day, sons and daughters of all ages around the world are being molded. Some are shaped for success, others for struggle.

At forty years old, Don was one of those struggling sons. He sat across from me, splayed out in the overstuffed chair of my summer office, a screened porch on the back of my house. Don had just finished lamenting about his three failed hair salons, two divorces, and ruined finances. Talk about feeling chewed up, spit out, and stomped on.

Don ran his hands through his thick hair. "What do I do? Just tell me what to do and I'll do it." He was used to calling the shots, but now he found himself falling into despair.

I let his plea sit there for a moment and then asked, "Tell me about growing up with your father. One-on-one, what was life like?"

His incredulous glare could have wilted the plants that surround us. "What does *that* have to do with my business problems?"

"Humor me," I replied gently.

Resigned, he thought for a few moments. He bowed his head and began to cry. Then crying turned into shoulder-shaking sobs.

Apparently, his father *did* have something to do with it.

In our meetings that followed, Don wept through boxes of tissues as memories came flooding back to him. He described times when his Dad didn't show up, wouldn't help with schoolwork, laughed at him, or always had to be right. Nothing Don did as a boy, or even now as an adult, was ever good enough for his old man.

"Not that it matters anyway," he said. "I've always done life without him. I don't need him now."

From the way he talked and the look on his face, it was evident that it hurt him to say those words, as if he had never said them out loud and doing so made it all the more real—all the more final.

Sorting through the anguish of his past, Don came to realize this broken relationship with his father was at the root of his present problems: personal, family, and business. Don hated his father, and worse yet, he knew he was like him in so many ways. The very ways his father had hurt him growing up, the things he did and said, were the things Don was doing to his employees, his family, and himself.

* * *

I wish I could say Don was a unique client, but people don't usually reach out for help until they're at rock bottom. It shouldn't be this way, but it is. Like a five-year-old child, we're prone to insist: "I don't need help. I can do it myself."

We may age, but we don't change as much as we like to think we do.

Even when clients know they need help, they're still looking for the quick and easy, step by step, tried and true recipe for success—and they want it now! Those steps don't exist, and there is no recipe.

Don's story is not uncommon. We all know stories like this or have parallels of our own. Over my lifetime, I've had many careers: seventeen years as a school teacher, two years as a principal, eleven years as a pastor, and several more years in my own private businesses. Each has provided a unique lens into the influence fathers have on our lives. I am also the son of a father and a father myself.

But it was my most recent fifteen-year-career as a personal and business life coach that shed fresh light on the father influence dynamic—a phenomenon that could not be ignored.

Like Don, the majority of my clients were business owners trying to navigate a struggling and unsustainable situation. They were coming to me for help with business issues, but inevitably the problems nearly always pointed back to the root of father absence, typically for generations.

Dealing with the *father relationship* first more often than not solved their *business issues.* The two are inextricably linked, usually to the client's surprise but no longer to mine.

Failings in relationships, school, finances, work, health, and family life are only some of the bitter fruit of father absence. And this phenomenon exists far beyond the arena of business, as was Don's experience. But it was finding the effect of fatherlessness in this strange setting that made it real to me in a whole new way, and compelled me to seek out new avenues of positive impact that I had never even considered before.

The truth is, it doesn't matter if you are a father or not, a man or a woman, if you were close to your father or never knew him—fatherhood affects your life and the lives of those you love. Father *presence* or *absence* is at work on every level of society.

It affects an individual's well-being, it affects a family's dynamics, and it affects a community's culture. Whether we know it or not, whether we like it or not, fatherhood affects us all.

This leads us to a story of fatherhood on the other side of the world.

Chapter 2

The Story of Ukraine

"No one enters existence as a spectator.
We either take up the life to which we have been
consecrated or we traitorously defect from it."

−EUGENE PETERSON

In 2005, I began volunteering with a local non-profit in Minnesota called the National Fathering Ministry with a street name of DadsFirst, as in *Dad's first responsibility is to his family.*

Our primary role is to work with dads and, in essence, teach them how to be strong fathers and involved husbands. There are many organizations that do this but, for me, DadsFirst goes deeper and addresses the heart of the matter. DadsFirst acknowledges that both suffering and joy are rooted in the father-child relationship.

DadsFirst expanded its outreach to Ukraine and, in October of 2006, I joined director Chuck Aycock and another board member for a two-week trip to Kyiv, Ukraine. By this time, Chuck had made the trip several times and had already established a similar organization there. We flew the eight-and-a-half hours across the Atlantic to Amsterdam and, after a two-hour layover, a final three-and-a-half-hour leg to our destination.

I'll never forget that first descent.

The international airport is located in Boryspil, a smaller town just east of Kyiv. The Ukrainian pronunciation sounds like "keev" as opposed to the more familiar two-syllable Russian, "key-ev." The countryside is a beautiful patchwork of land. Each village house hosts a garden large enough for families to grow food for a whole year. Beyond these family plots were barren farm fields running for miles, with no barns or farm homes in sight. Ghost fields.

I learned that these ghost fields were a holdover from the years of Communism and the heavy hand of Joseph Stalin and his regime. Collective farming gradually became a military-enforced takeover by the Soviet regime and required peasants and farmers to surrender their assets—land, crops, livestock, food reserves, even their homes—in exchange for communes. This takeover exacerbated a natural famine creating a man-made famine known as Holodomor, *murder by starvation,* which killed millions of Ukrainians.[1]

At the time of my visit, fifteen years into an independent Ukraine, the fields remained largely untouched. The condition of the land was just a taste of the history that shaped the culture I was about to witness.

As I waited to pass through customs, agents dressed in military-like garb inspected passports, luggage, and people before allowing passage into the country. My stomach turned with nervous energy as I watched them question travelers. Not all the outcomes were positive.

Eventually, it was my turn. I gave the agent my passport and form. He took his time, scrutinizing my documents—and me.

"Vwy arre you cohming to Ukrrraine?" The agent's deep voice enveloped his thick accent and rolled Rs. His staunch military attire, paired with stoic expression, was intimidating—even for a grown man with nothing to hide. I half expected him to say, "Arrest zis man."

In spite of the cool day, sweat trickled down my back. "I'm here on business."

"Vwat is your biznezz?"

"We teach men how to be fathers and husbands." That didn't really sound like a business matter, but it was the truth. I hoped it would pass the test.

He seemed surprised, and his strict formality allowed a thin smile. "Guud. Vwe need zat."

My rapid exhale must have been audible. "Spaseba," I managed to say, though I was not entirely sure of my pronunciation. Russian for *thank you*.

The guard smiled a little more and waved me through with my passport.

Going through customs is rarely a comfortable experience, but I was sure the trip would be a picnic in comparison.

On day three, we had a particularly engaging interaction at a big University in Kyiv. We were invited to give a presentation to a class of sociology majors preparing to become social workers. There were 110 students, all young women save for four young men sitting (hiding?) in the back, and a few professors and administrators in the front row. The room was large enough to hold three times as many.

So many buildings in Ukraine were built with soviet architecture. High ceilings, large single-pane windows with thin, expansive white curtains, creaky wood floors, and walls in need of scraping and fresh paint. No media equipment, only walls of chalkboards and a few pictures or charts. Despite the warm and balmy weather outside, the thick concrete walls radiated a bitter cold that forced us to don our jackets whenever we went inside.

The faces in the audience reflected curiosity and even excitement about what they might hear from us. It was like a field trip for them. They had not been briefed on our topic, and we had ninety minutes.

Sasha, our Ukrainian Executive Director, introduced himself and gave the name of the organization. Then he got more personal and shared about his family, his wife, and three daughters: what they all do, how they relate, and the kinds of things they do together. He described them as a beautiful bouquet of flowers. The students and faculty expressed rapt attention, even amazement, as if they were hearing a love story they could only imagine.

Sasha then introduced Chuck and me, and we took our turn describing our families, kids and grandkids, work, and hobbies and interests. Even through Ukrainian translators, our descriptions kept them engaged. The room glowed with bright faces and easy smiles.

We shifted into our message in our familiar style—trading off, interjecting to complement what each other was saying, and injecting a good bit of humor. We invited the students to ask questions or share comments at any time, letting them know we wanted to hear what they had to say. While this team-teaching approach is familiar to us, it was a new phenomenon to them. At every school we visited, teachers and administrators talked about it and the impression it made on them. The norm at that time in Ukraine was for the professors to rule and protect their space—they lecture, students listen, and no one else speaks. Another holdover of ingrained culture, and not the last.

Sasha drew a large circle on the chalkboard. "If this represents the family, where on the diagram would you place the mother?"

Without hesitation they responded as one, "In the center."

"Very good." He placed an X in the center. "Now, where would you place the father?"

The silence was deafening.

Finally, a lone voice said, as if we ought to know, "He's not in the family."

Sasha was ready. "So, you are saying he is outside the circle?"

"Yes," they responded in chorus once again.

"Okay. For discussion purposes, let's assume he is at least like Sputnik, circling the family." He put an X on the circle. They seemed to agree with that description.

Next, Chuck shared our observations of the culture from the previous day. The city came alive in the evening. The streets, restaurants, transportation, and activities were packed with young people, making it easy for us to observe.

First, he strutted around mimicking the young women, smartly dressed, shoulders back, chin up, and acting with intention. The males, on the other hand, were so casual in their presence. Their posture and behavior made one wonder if they had an interest in women or any testosterone at all. When he mimicked the boys' lackadaisical behavior, the entire room laughed and nodded in agreement. He even got a rise out of the four boys in the back. His impersonations were right on.

That's how it is in Ukraine—it's all about the mother. She runs the family, and the father is left out of most everything except procreation and handing over his paycheck. Even the dating and flirtations of the young reflect such expectations. Like the ghost fields, this behavior, too, is a holdover from the days of Communism and Stalin. Every generation is groomed to continue the practice.

The students knew about the atrocities and philosophies of the past, but hadn't connected them with the behaviors and family structures of today. A lot of *aha* moments reflected in their faces. The professors were just as amazed. We were not telling them anything new; we were simply connecting the dots.

As the bell rang signaling the end of our ninety minutes, an administrator stood up. "This is too important to end now. You can all stay if our presenters are willing to continue for another ninety minutes."

We were, and every student stayed. This was a moment of huge confirmation for us.

We spent the next ninety minutes explaining the traditional roles of the father and mother and what happens to the children when these roles are not allowed to happen and how it impacts generations. We backed our teaching with extensive research done in Ukraine, although the results were similar to that of the United States.

The most common stories from the students revolved around fathers leaving the country to find work. Absentee fathers are all too common. Even when they are in the home, it is typical for them to be inactive in family life, making them, in essence, absent fathers. Involved fathering is a new and unknown role for the majority of the population in Ukraine.

One student in the room said she could now understand how important it was for the father to partner in the family. She had a boyfriend and was going to ask him that day how he saw his role as a father. If he did not want to be an involved father and husband, she promised to dump him and find one who would. Several others chimed in their agreement and made similar promises. They got it!

At the end of the three hours, Sasha asked again where the father belonged on the family diagram.

Everyone agreed in unison, "In the center, next to the mother!"

* * *

Despite this fun interaction, we couldn't help but be discouraged at the systemic influence of fatherlessness in Ukrainian society. The majority of trained social workers we talked to felt powerless to confront the ingrained status quo for men. We did feel encouraged that at least *these* hundred-plus young students now had a new mindset that would begin to make a difference.

Over the next eight years, I made this same trip a total of twelve times, staying two weeks each time. Every trip was filled with powerful observations and interactions like this. But every time I came home, it was impossible to ignore the understanding that fatherlessness is not unique to Ukraine.

Despite a vastly different history and culture, father absence plagues large sectors of our population, too. In fact, the United States is officially reported to be the most fatherless nation in the world, and whether we want to recognize it or not, we do know it to be true.[2] Over 90 percent of parents acknowledge that there is a father absence crisis in America—one that exists across every socioeconomic class.[3]

Recognizing this truth is step one.

Step two is taking ownership for ourselves and future generations by understanding our past and understanding the insidious nature of father absence. Alongside this, we must also embrace the true power of father involvement and claim it for ourselves and our society—not as a luxury, but as a requirement for humanity to thrive.

Chapter 3

Defining Father Presence and Absence

"An engaged and loving father is the most powerful man-making force on the planet. The opposite is also true. When fathers are absent, physically or emotionally, the wound that results is profound."

—EARL HIPP, AUTHOR

pres·ence [1]
/'prez'ns/
noun
the state of existing, occurring, or being present.
a person that exists or is present in a place but is not seen.

ab·sence [2]
/'abs'ns/
noun
the state of being away from a place or person.
an occasion of being away from a place or person.
the non existence or lack of being.

Consider for a moment the true difference between being present and being absent. There is no greater divide between two things. They are opposite in every way. One is and one is not. Now consider these concepts in relation to fathering.

Father presence. Father absence.

Fathering has been a part of human life for everyone, including you. From before you were born, whether you are a son or a daughter, whether your father was present or absent, your father and his father before him have each contributed to and influenced realities about your life, your family, and even your society. It's taken the course of my life to become aware and receptive to this all-encompassing influence.

With this awareness, it's now impossible to be anything but an impassioned advocate for strong child-father relationships at all ages.

Clarity First

Let us take a moment to define exactly what we mean by father presence and father absence. At DadsFirst, we teach that there are four types of father influence:

- Physical—being around each other in person, living in the same house

- Emotional—affirming, saying and showing "I love you"

- Psychological—modeling identity and roles of men and fathers

- Spiritual—understanding and leading children's values and beliefs

For our purposes, I will group them into two distinct forms of connection:

1. Physical—the father and child's physical proximity

2. Relational—the emotional, psychological, and spiritual proximity between a father and child

To more clearly represent the dynamics of these connections, we can look at how a train is connected.

In a passenger train, cars are physically held together by a coupler. This coupler represents the physical connection between a father and his child.

Along with the coupler, there are power lines that control the brakes and pass the electricity from one car to the next. This represents the father's relational connection with his child.

Among these two forms of connection, we can identify four distinct father-child scenarios:

1. The Present Father—Physically present (coupled) and involved (connected)

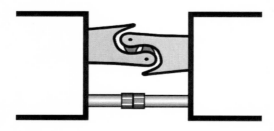

2. The Involved Father—Absent (uncoupled) but still involved (connected)

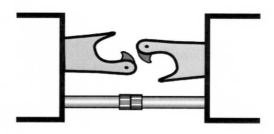

3. The Passive Father—Physically present (coupled) but uninvolved (disconnected)

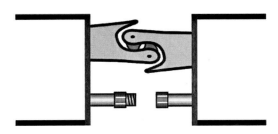

4. The Absent Father—Physically absent (uncoupled) and uninvolved (disconnected)

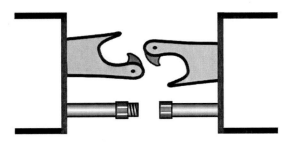

Each of these scenarios represent a mode of fathering. Even absence is still a form of fathering, because his influence never ceases to exist in the life of his child—at any age, for better or worse.

With that in mind, let's look at each of these fathering scenarios in greater depth.

The Present Father

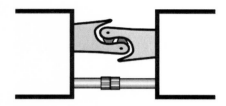

Physically Present and Involved. This is the ideal, the goal. It is the reality children hope for, even expect, to have dad choose them over other options in his life. For dad to both be there and be involved is the most likely scenario for healthy, balanced people from childhood through adulthood for generations.

You might notice, as I have, that two-parent families, and involved fathers in particular, are disappearing from society. In 1960, 88 percent of all families were two-parent families. In 2016, the figure had slipped to 69 percent.[3] Although the majority will agree that fathers are the mainstay of our nation, few people will stand up and say it.

I challenge the reader to notice—movie after movie, as part of news events, written into books, and occurring in neighborhood scenarios—how often the father wound is at the core of the holes and wounds we all have in our hearts.

Yes, being involved when absent is possible. But involvement is so much easier and attainable when the father is right there at home connecting to his wife and children on an ongoing basis. His presence affects not only relationships within the family, but also its financial stability, health, education, opportunities, and extended relationships, as we'll see in chapter 5. Being physically present and involved also says to each family member, "I choose you."

The Involved Father

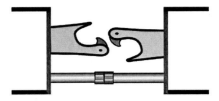

Physically Absent but Still Involved. Surprisingly, this category is second best. Being physically absent from home is often a necessity to provide for the family. However, that does not necessarily require being uninvolved from the lives of family members, especially in today's world of technology. The next chapter compares the stories of two boys, each with physically absent fathers—one who has chosen to be involved with his son and one who has not.

The main consideration is whether the father finds creative, alternative ways to stay involved in the lives of his children despite physical distance. Often, the problem is lack of perspective. We feel trapped by our circumstances, like there is no way out. We *have* to be gone.

I often hear the excuse, "But I have to be gone in order to have a job." The father who chooses his children will seek and find ways to be creatively involved no matter what.

The Passive Father

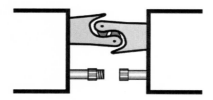

Physically Present but Uninvolved. The Passive Father is far worse. This category describes my client Don. Don's father was physically present but uninvolved emotionally, psychologically, and spiritually. He was at home and had access to his wife and his son but was not involved in their lives. This may describe men who invest long hours into work every day but then are too busy, too tired, or have given their attention away. They're too involved elsewhere, mentally or physically, to be involved in the activities, interests, or lives of their own children.

They use their circumstances to justify their choices. Or they may feel it is not their job, interest, or within their ability to be involved. They might even say it is the job of the mother and school to raise their kids. Others may be too self-absorbed or consumed by various addictions.

I am convinced this is the most dangerous category of the four because it is so subtle and widespread. It is hidden. If the father is physically present at home, we tend to assume it is a strong balanced family. In reality, this setting leaves an impact that is identical to that of a physically absent father. His uninvolvement ensures similar outcomes.

While passivity may be a result of psychosomatic symptoms or factors of mental illness, I believe it's primarily a learned behavior—a passive father learns to be passive by watching and learning from his own passive father, or he learns it in the process of being self-absorbed by a lack of motivation, lack of caring for others (selfishness), or not understanding his role and responsibility as a person and a father.

There is, however, a difference between the passive father and the uninvolved father in that a passive father ought to at least provide a better level of income, health care, and protection for the family than if he is both uninvolved and absent.

The Absent Father

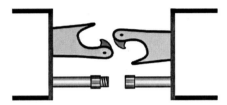

Physically Absent and Uninvolved. This is the worst option of all. These might be fathers who have been divorced from their family, were kicked out, picked up and left, or are absent due to work, travel, incarceration, or death. These fathers are not connected to or involved with their families.

I can't tell you how many men going through our ten-lesson program in DadsFirst fit this category, both as sons and as fathers themselves. These men didn't just dislike their fathers, they *hated* them. They were glad their dads were out of their lives—or at least that is what they said. Yet, as I observed their deep anger, I also witnessed a little boy peeking out with the hope and desire that their dad might really be the hero they always wanted him to be.

Sons and daughters become defensive about absent dads in order to convince themselves that they are alright or better off without them. This response also justifies themselves as the same kind of father, if in different ways, to their own children. They become the absent and uninvolved father that they hate so much.

This was the most common experience for men in halfway houses—those transitioning from prison or treatment centers. But the reality is that many of the men in our seminars at churches and corporations presented the *same* anger and the *same* experiences. Dad simply wasn't around and wasn't involved. This is so common it has become accepted as the norm by many. Single mother families are so prevalent in today's age that they are assumed to be normal. Many of this generation of "kids" don't get angry, they just accept it. Others develop an anger that seethes under the surface.

In many ways, we have become a world of angry young men and disappointed, frustrated young women. What they don't realize is that so much of their struggle with purpose, identity, esteem, fulfillment, anger, and poor choices, has its roots in dad's absence and uninvolvement.

The Scope of the Problem

According to the United States Census figures, nearly 19.7 million children were living in absent father homes in 2019.[4] That's one out of every four children in America (26 percent). The figures break down further to be one in four white children (24 percent), 4 in 10 Latino children (41 percent), and nearly one in two African American children (48.5 percent).[5] When considering this specific definition of fatherlessness, the United States is the most fatherless nation in the world.[6][7]

When we consider the largely unquantifiable number of uninvolved fathers who technically live with their children, it can be difficult to measure the true scope of the father crisis.

What is clear are the 93 percent of mothers and 91 percent of fathers who say we have a father absence crisis in America.[8] But just because it is obvious that we have a problem, it doesn't mean the *specific* problem we have is clear.

The first step in any solution is examining the problem with specificity and comprehension in order to ensure we truly know what we're dealing with.

Chapter 4

Recognizing Uninvolved Fathers

"Man is not what he thinks he is, he is what he hides."
—ANDRÉ MALRAUX, AUTHOR

"If it is important to you, you will find a way. If not, you'll find an excuse."
—ANONYMOUS

Absent fathers occur in every sector and level of society—from the poor to the rich, from uneducated to well-schooled, throughout the nonprofit, for-profit, and public servant worlds, throughout cultures and races, and from blue collar workers to CEOs and owners of businesses. And the negative effects of absent fathers occur in every sector as well. Consequences care nothing for demographics.

The trouble with the absent father statistic is that it does not account for one very essential aspect of fathering: the power connection. This represents emotional, psychological, and spiritual involvement. A father may be physically absent, but as we will infer from the many statistics coming in chapter 5, if he is emotionally uninvolved, the impact on the child is equal to having an absent father. The National Center for Fatherhood has stated how significant this issue is. "If it were classified as a disease, fatherlessness would be an epidemic worthy of attention as a national emergency." [1]

Two Ukrainian Boys:
Same Woods, Different Paths Taken

While visiting Ukraine, we talked with a class of high school seniors. There was one young man who appeared unengaged, laughing about things we said, making joking comments to his friends and in general, saying no to our topic. But he wasn't fooling us. He would fit the description of one who had developed a "swaggering, intimidating persona in an attempt to disguise their underlying fears, resentments, anxieties, and unhappiness."[2]

We directed a question straight to him about his relationship with his father. He told us that his father has always worked in another country, so he never sees him. He said with an air of apparent defiance, "I don't need my father. I can do life without him."

Because his father is gone and does not reach out to him, there is no chance for a relationship, and the boy's understanding is that the father has no choice and neither does he and that's just the way it is. This scenario is a reality for many children in Ukraine. Men often go elsewhere, in and out of the country, to find work.

This young man gave the impression of a person without a strong character who needed to resort to those behaviors to find acceptance and confidence. But it was a facade. The boy was wearing masks, one to hide his anger and sense of abandonment and a second to appear as if those facts were not true and didn't matter even if they were.

I believe this boy, regardless of his aloof attitude, felt angry and rejected and was trying to make up for his father's absence in his own way. Without knowing it, his reactions were establishing behavior and patterns in response to the fact that his father had chosen something other than him. His behaviors were a response to abandonment.

A World of Difference

Later the same day, at a different school, we talked to a boy in another class of high school seniors. But this young man was a direct contrast compared to the first. He was well dressed, engaged in dialogue, polite, intelligent, and exuding self-confidence. It was obvious he had a lot of friends in the class, and he was respectful in how he related to us. Turns out, he was the president of his class, to boot.

He also told us that his father had to leave home for a foreign country in order to find work. Strikingly similar story, but with one major difference: his father called him and his family on the telephone almost every evening and talked to them long-distance.

He described how every year his father took him to work for a week or two at a time just to be together. While there, his father showed him what he does for work and what his life is like outside of work in this distant city. In addition to that, he spent one or two weeks a year vacationing with his father.

So here we see two boys whose fathers have the same circumstances for work, but the fathers' responses are totally different. One blames the circumstances, uses it as an excuse, and stays uninvolved, running from his strengths as a father. The other finds ways to creatively stay involved with his son. We also see that the first son is not developing the self-confidence, self-worth, and identity that we know comes through the father or a good father figure.

Even though they have different personalities, the impact of these absent fathers is evident. While not always this conclusive, this outcome is typical.

The Depths of Uninvolvement

A passive father has the potential of an overwhelming negative effect when compounded with things like drug and alcohol abuse, and/or physical and emotional abuse. While there are some statistics on this type of abuse, much goes unreported and undetected. Once again, when the father is present, it is often assumed that life is okay. This is the monstrous setting for domestic abuse, which so often goes unaddressed until it escalates to injuries or in many cases, death.

Fathers who are overly absent due to the demands of their work aren't often associated with the term *absent father*. However, to a developing child, the impact of the absence is the same. In fact, being absent physically most or all the time for work purposes has many of the same effects on a child as being absent for less glamorous reasons, like divorce, crime, addiction, or abandonment.

The death of a father actually has less impact on a child than all these other excuses. Why is that? In the case of death, the child subconsciously understands there was no choice for or against them. It was out of their father's control. In all the other options, the father has some measure of choice. To the child, not being chosen over any of those options equates to being abandoned. They may not know that's what happened, but they do know the pain of it.

Hiding in Plain Sight

Author and psychotherapist Jeff VanVonderen describes a scenario in which a family is driving to church on a Sunday morning. [3]

As is typical of most of their daily lives, they are all fighting and bickering at each other, including dad. They arrive in the parking lot, get out of the car, and walk up to the door of the church.

An enthusiastic greeter opens the door with a big smile and happy handshake, asking, "How are you today?" to which dad and everyone else returns smiles and the automatic reply, "Fine, how are you?"

Nothing could be further from the truth, but everyone who sees this family assumes everything really is fine.

It isn't. It's a lie.

Jeff says church ought to be the one place we can go and be truthful about how hard it is for our family to get along, and for dad to really be the dad. Instead, we wear masks and refuse to deal with what's real.

Most outsiders look at a family and, if the father is present, assume the family is intact. And certainly, many are—but just as certainly, many are not.

The typical uninvolved father works all day, comes home, doesn't want to be bothered, tells his wife to keep the kids away, and then sits down for supper. After supper, he plops in front of the TV or some other pastime and goes to bed. He gets up in the morning and repeats the sequence, or some variety of it. He's home, but disengaged emotionally and mentally from his family, especially his kids. He may make promises to show up at athletic or music events or even birthdays, but his work or other distractions typically end up winning his attention.

Such fathers know very little about their children and do not communicate well with them or with their spouses.

I remember one concerned father I talked to in Ukraine (although it could as well have been in the US) who asked for advice on how to work with young people in his church.

I asked, "What do they say when you talk to them?"

"Talk to them?" he replied, "Why would I talk to them?"

Men often feel ill-equipped to relate to any children of any age, including their own. They may also believe that, as parents, they are to direct their children rather than engage them. This type of absence is harder to detect but can be equally felt.

In My Case

My own father was thirty years old when I came along. I was his second born, so he had a few years of practice by then. As a devoted family man, he was home most evenings and weekends.

Despite this, he was not what I would call an involved father. There is a difference between being devoted to your role as the family provider and being devoted to your role as a dad. The former merely checks the box. The latter not only checks it, but constructs it.

It was mom who knew what was going on in my life and made the majority of our family's decisions. I remember, as a high school kid, being so resentful of her strict conservative control.

Now, as a mature adult, I can look back at that time and see it for what it really was. Dad was there, but he really wasn't. He had forfeited his parenting role to mom. Her overt control was really her way to cope with a parenting partner who opted out of his essential role. She had to bear the majority of the weight of keeping the household under control, so she did. With this realization, the resentment that I had for my mother lifted somewhat and shifted to my father. He may have been there physically, but he decided not to be my pal, my hero, my role model, my dad.

Recognizing Our Roots

In my work over the years, I've talked about fatherlessness to countless men, women, families, and business owners. Often, when I get to the part about passive fathering, I see the light bulbs come on. This language allows people to put a name and description to what they have experienced with their own fathers or seen in many others. When men come to this realization about their own fathers, they usually begin to recognize elements of passivity in themselves.

Passivity begins as a very subtle way to manipulate life around us. We don't think we are able to handle the roles we find ourselves in and find ways to rationalize or make excuses to not show up. Many men are passive because they grew up with a mom who took care of them like their personal maid, and they still expect the same from their wives as grown men. However, men also have the capacity to recognize their behavior and to choose their response. Except perhaps in the case of mental illness, everyone is responsible—that is, able to respond. Unfortunately, most *choose* to react, hide, or selfishly choose themselves instead.

If we can hide, we push away the responsibilities that come with our roles. We can disappear or zone out. Then when pressure comes our way, we don't have to show up or be the person we were made to be.[4] Hiding often takes the form of behaviors that easily turn into addiction, including anything from drugs and alcohol to TV, eating, working out, golf, even rationalization of our behavior—anything used to avoid letting our strengths show up. And by "strengths," I mean all those factors that are a part of our unique make-up.

Of course, there is also the element of fear and selfishness. I have heard many men explain that they do not know how to be a father or parent, so they leave it to their kids' mother. Others have said they don't even want to have kids because they don't know how to raise them or don't want to bring them into today's world. After their own negative experiences as a child, they don't want to subject their own kids to the same pain. And then there is a growing number of men who simply say they want to do their own thing and don't desire to be tied down by having children.

There are legitimate reasons for not having children, but for most, that choice reflects the generational sense of father passivity that produces fear and selfishness. Rather than understanding where such a choice originates, it becomes a lie that hides our real excuses, values, fears, and selfishness.

Yes, it is true that a man may simply be a quiet, introverted personality, but there is a difference between that and passivity that avoids involvement or ignores the other factors around him that he knows are causing relational problems. In such a case, to claim it is due to being a quiet introvert is to use the trait as an excuse, a shield, or better yet, a mask to hide behind.

This hiding may be due to frustration, not knowing how to respond, or even embarrassment around not doing the appropriate thing. But regardless of the reasons for being uninvolved, the fact is that it creates significant and lasting damage.

Passivity isn't captured in a census poll and may well make up a larger group than those fathers in the US who are physically absent from the home (26 percent). This makes it all the more a worrisome, tragic, and sinister problem. At least when dad is physically gone, everyone knows he is gone.

Due to its hidden nature, few people recognize passive fathering at work or understand how negatively impacting it is. As a society, we often justify passive fathering as "the way things are," an equally toxic version of "boys will be boys." But the impact is real and cannot be ignored.

One man I interviewed from a family business had such a response. He was quiet and reserved in his demeanor (passive) and was already retired, leaving other siblings and even his father still running the business. While saying he was content with his decision to retire, his anger, frustration, and disappointment was evident—lying just beneath the surface. Rather than being content, I realized he was simply resigned to the fact the family business had not been a good experience. His indirect words indicated the family relationships were in shambles. Any comments from me about family dynamics or reconciliation were brushed aside as so much dust on the shelf. He passively reflected, "That's just the way things are, and I'm not about to rock the boat"

But there is a light to this dark tunnel—the impact of fathering is a two-way street. As negative as absence is, presence is just as positive.

Chapter 5

A Father's Impact

"A hero is a man who is afraid to run away."

—ENGLISH PROVERB

It is said that marriage is a major confrontation to the single life. Well, having a child is a major confrontation to the married life without kids. I became a father when I was twenty-two years old. I remember thinking about how this new role was impacting and *impeding* my life. After all, I was a man with important places to be, with grown up (and not so grown up) things to do.

When I was struggling through those first few years of being a dad, I noticed there was a spattering of men who appeared to be really great dads. There were also many men who seemed like me—ignorant, unsure, unaware, and immature.

It took a while for me to break free of that mentality, to truly understand how much impact my mindset and my actions would have on the lives of my wife and children. I'm grateful to be free of those self-centered mindsets, as free as any human can be, but to be honest, this task has taken a lifetime to achieve. Researchers Pleck and Masciadrelli give a more scientific explanation for my experience.

A person's continuous, healthy development depends on being exposed during each period [of brain development] to people who provide nurturance and safe love, people who themselves live out of a higher brain and a bigger vision of life. We need models of higher development around us to move forward.[1]

One of the best lessons a person can learn is just how much the mode and method of fathering shapes our world—individuals, families, communities, and culture—in significant, generational ways.

The Power of Presence and Involvement

Before we can fully understand the problem and prescribe solutions to the absent father crisis, we need to look fully at what it means for a father to be present. What does involved fathering look like? What are the benefits for children, families, society, and equally important, the father himself?

Most studies focus on the benefits of involved fathers to their children in the first twelve years of life. But in my experience, the impact of involved fathers, both positive and negative, can be witnessed at every age: pre-birth to twelve, teenagers, young adults, middle-agers, and retirees. I can't stress it enough: the impact of the father lasts for a lifetime. For each father, it began generations ago and will continue for generations to come. Fathers have every opportunity to influence that impact.

Let's take a look at some results of studies and quotes from researchers who are also interested in the impact of the father and what it means to be involved.

Gestation, Birth, and Infancy

- When fathers are involved during the pregnancy, babies have fewer complications—especially those leading to premature births—including anemia, chronic high blood pressure, eclampsia, and placental abruption.[2]

- The father's involvement during pregnancy can affect the levels of cortisol in the mother which in sustained doses can weaken the child's developing brain architecture.[3]

- Dad's attendance is more than a mere gesture of support and commitment—it's a window into the health and well-being of mother and child.[4]

- Premature infants who have increased visits from their fathers during hospitalization tend to have improved weight gain and score higher on developmental tests.[5]

- Absent fathers are three times more likely to have children with health complications as early as three months after the birth. They are also more likely to have children born underweight. Moms who are unaccompanied by the father at birth are more likely to have experienced complications during pregnancy or at the time of birth.[6]

- Trust is learned (or not) in the first six months of life. The father's interaction is a primary factor in that learning.[7]

Children

- Children living with their married biological or adoptive parents have better access to health care than children living in any other family type.[8]

- A study found that children with highly involved fathers are more confident and less anxious when placed in unfamiliar settings. These children are better able to deal with frustration, as well as adapt to changing circumstances and breaks from their routine. They are also better equipped with a sense of independence and an identity outside the mother-child relationship.[9]

According to a study investigating paternal and youth involvement, the greater the father's involvement, the lower the level of adolescent behavior problems both in terms of aggression and antisocial behavior and negative feelings such as anxiety, depression, and low self-esteem.[10]

Adults

- The greatest predictor of whether or not a child grows into an adult who demonstrates "empathic concern" is whether or not his/her father is involved in their childcare.[11]

- Adult mothers benefit from the responsible care taken by fathers in a variety of ways. Statistics show that the child-mother attachment is more secure when child-father attachment is secure, and that positive mother-child relationships are most often linked with positive father-child relationships.[12]

- Adult fathers benefit from their own involvement as well, better coping well with stressful situations and everyday hassles and feeling confident they have a lot to offer others in terms of their job skills, parenting skills, and social relationships.[13]

- The responsible care taken by fathers for themselves, their children and the mother of their children lends itself to a higher level of care outside of the immediate family as well. Studies show that men who actively participate in their children's lives are also more likely to be directly involved in their community, to serve in civic community leadership positions, and to attend church services.[14]

Society

The impact of father presence is easily witnessed within the foster care system:

- When non-resident fathers are involved, there is a higher likelihood the child will leave foster care and be reunited with their family. In turn, this makes it less likely that parental rights will be terminated and the child placed for adoption.[15]

- Children with highly involved non-resident fathers are discharged from foster care more quickly than those with less or no involvement.[16]

- When children leave foster care and are reunified with their family, usually to live with their mother, higher levels of non-resident father involvement are associated with a substantially lower likelihood of subsequent maltreatment allegations.[17]

The Impact of Absence and Uninvolvement

There is a great deal of research that has documented the importance of fathering by examining the negative effects of father absence.

Children

- Children from fatherless homes are more likely to perform more poorly on standardized tests in school assignments, drop out of school, be sexually active, or become susceptible to disease, psychosomatic health symptoms, and illnesses such as acute and chronic pain, asthma, headaches, stomach aches, and STDs.[18]

- When their fathers are not involved in their lives, children report feeling abandoned, struggling with their emotions and episodic bouts of self-loathing. They become more susceptible to peer pressures resulting in anxiety, depression, and suicide.[19]

- Fatherless homes result in children who are five times more likely to have experienced physical abuse and emotional maltreatment, with a 100-times higher risk of fatal abuse; additionally, preschoolers not living with both of their biological parents are forty times more likely to be sexually abused.[20]

Adolescents and Teenagers

- According to the National Center on Addiction and Substance Abuse at Columbia University, a comparison of twelve- to thirteen-year-olds who have five or more family dinners per week, those in the same age group who didn't are six times more likely to have used marijuana, more than four-and-a-half times likelier to have used tobacco, and more than two-and-a-half times likelier to have used alcohol.[21]

- In response to father absence, many adolescents develop a swaggering, intimidating persona in an attempt to disguise their underlying fears, resentments, anxieties, and unhappiness. Additionally, adolescent girls often manifest a desire for male connection and become susceptible to exploitation by adult men.[22]

- Fatherless homes are the predicted source of [23]

  - 63 percent of youth suicides

  - 90 percent of all homeless and runaway children

  - 85 percent of all children that exhibit behavioral disorders

  - 80 percent of rapists motivated by displaced anger

  - 71 percent of all high school dropouts

  - 70 percent of juveniles in state-operated institutions

  - 85 percent of all youths sitting in prison

Adults

- Divorce often leads to absence and uninvolvement of the father in childhood. This impacts children long beyond childhood and well into adulthood in ways that are far more damaging than modern society likes to admit. Being a child of divorce is real trauma that many adults do not recognize or resolve.[24]

- Young adults who had a parent incarcerated during their childhood are more likely to skip needed healthcare, smoke cigarettes, engage in risky sexual behaviors, and abuse alcohol and drugs.[25] The impact on a child lasts a lifetime.

- Adults who were raised without a father are more likely to [26] [27] [28]

    - suffer from poverty

    - receive welfare

    - marry early

    - have children out of wedlock

    - divorce

    - commit delinquent acts

    - engage in drug and alcohol use and smoke

    - not attain academic and professional qualifications in adulthood

    - offend and go to jail as adults

    - experience unemployment, have low incomes, remain on social assistance, and experience homelessness

Society

The impact of absence goes beyond the life of the individual, beyond that of the family, and into society as a whole for generations to come. Father absence results in an element of trauma. Not having the father fulfill his security roles of protector and provider results in an increased level of stress, both physical and mental. This has been shown in a federally funded study called *Fragile Families and Child Wellbeing Study* that speaks to the reality that absence impacts DNA.[29]

Chromosomes in DNA have protective caps on the ends called telomeres that keep them from deteriorating. Scientists believe the telomeres are linked directly to health and life span. The study shows the ends of the chromosomes in children who have experienced father loss are cut short, contributing to a wide range of traumatic consequences.

Different kinds of father loss make a difference in the amount of telomere loss, with an average of 14 percent compared to those with a father in the home. The impact on boys is the greatest, with the loss jumping to 40 percent of the telomeres as compared to girls. There was no difference in regards to ethnicity.

While the telomeres carryout genetic code, the study indicates they are also affected by all kinds of trauma in life and, in effect, are listening to the input they receive. Because of that, the scientists believe the length of telomeres could increase with diet, exercise, appropriate sleep, and an overall more peaceful lifestyle.

The Need for a Solution

Such information and statistics represent some hard realities for us as individuals and as a society. Often, rather than dealing with such truths, we run from them. We dismiss, we discredit. We justify it away.

It's not a big deal. Kids are resilient.

They're still being taken care of.

It was the same with my father.

Maybe this isn't you, but it is likely something you've heard before.

Yes, kids are resilient, thank God, but consider three things:

- Whether a father is away for work or sitting in prison, the impact of his absence on his children is the same.
- Though children grow into adults, the impact of an uninvolved father continues their entire lives—affecting their schooling, work performance, finances, relationships, and emotional well-being.
- Unless intentional action is taken to stop the cycle, the effects of an absent father will likely pass on for generations.

In *Fatherless America*, David Blankenhorn calls the crisis of fatherless children "the most destructive trend of our generation."

We know that father absence is the most critical social issue of our time because the majority of social problems correlate more strongly with fatherlessness than with *any other factor,* surpassing race, social class, and poverty. A recent British report from the University of Birmingham, *Dad and Me*, confirms this, concluding that the need for a father is on an epidemic scale, and that "father deficit" should be treated as a public health issue.[30]

I have talked with teachers and administrators about the importance and impact of fathers, and they agree wholeheartedly. And yet, when frustrated with school violence, behavior, and learning issues, they rarely introduce the subject of fathers as a solution.

We must face the issue with eyes wide open because it's only then that we can truly chart a course for positive change. The nuance of father absence, the power of father presence, the scope of the absence epidemic, the astonishing impact absence and presence have on every sector of society—this is what matters most.

My mission is to transform absent fathers to present fathers whenever possible. And when it's not possible, to help the children of the absent father, who may be adults and parents themselves, to address and heal from the destructive patterns that father absence imposes.

My mission is to set families free—fathers, mothers, sons, and daughters. It is more than possible. You may not be able to see it yet, but there is hope.

Chapter 6

The Active Choice of Presence

"Every father should remember one day his son
will follow his example, not his advice."

—CHARLES KETTERING

My first real understanding of the effects of fatherlessness developed as I worked in the education system as a teacher and administrator. I was neck deep in interaction with children and their families.

Through it all, there was a single crystal-clear reality that presented itself time and time again: the powerful effect of fatherhood. Its presence or absence was consistently made evident through a child's posture, demeanor, attitudes, and behaviors.

As a school principal, fifth-grade twins Mark and Mike captured my attention. These boys were as shy and quiet as their mom, dad, and sister. But things began to change as they moved into sixth grade. Some rough, foul words, along with bold, brash comments were accompanied by actions that were becoming bullyish and rather alarming in the classroom, hallways, and on the playground. At the conference, mom started the conversation about some changes at home before I even brought up the boys' behavior. She was concerned that dad's job was affecting the family.

"May I share some observations?"

They both nodded, so I proceeded.

"Dad, I can guess what you do for work by watching your boys." My guess was right. "I, too, grew up in a construction family. What I know is that people in the trades often tend to develop a tough-guy, macho image exemplified by their language, swagger, habits, and lifestyle. Every kind of work has its own version of this. It is picked up by and rubbed off on most everyone on the job in order to fit in.

"And I have to say, the lingo and mannerisms from your work have rubbed off on you, and now the twins are picking it up. I don't think you would be too pleased if I were to be more explicit about their language and behavior."

Having told me her concerns, mom was understandably fidgety while I was talking so bluntly to them.

Dad, on the other hand, appeared embarrassed, more like a kid caught with his hand in the cookie jar. I could tell he knew I was right, and he agreed with me.

That conference was like a wakeup call with perfect timing for their family.

"Here's my challenge to you," I went on. "Decide now what you want for your children in terms of character qualities, values, personalities, self-esteem, and ethics—and understand that you will have to be the model of those traits if they are to become like your ideal for them. Set out to be the one who rubs off on others at work instead of being the rub-ee. Why is this important? Because whatever you become, your kids will become. Your choices now will shape them for life."

In the ensuing school year, those boys were just as vociferous and active, but what was obvious was their cleaned up language and behavior. Dad was at work in some powerful and effective ways at home. He told me later that it was having an effect at work, too. The change in his leadership focus had changed the whole dynamic of their family and the way they faced struggles together.

Make no doubt about it: fathers have an impact on us our entire lives, including when we go to work, get married, and raise our own kids. We must find ways to become aware of, understand, and deal with it for the sake of our own futures and those of our sons and daughters.

But What If It's Too Late?

In DadsFirst, we have a ten-lesson series that we deliver to different groups. Whether with ex-cons and rehab clients or at high-level corporations, the response often comes up, "My father died already. It's too late."

Some of you may be thinking it's too late as well. You believe your father or the father of your children is unreachable, whether physically or emotionally.

That is rarely the case.

Our response: "This is about you. It is about resolving your own personal identity and esteem issues. Go through the same procedures we use. Write your 'Dear Dad'[1] letter as one of the steps. Then either file it away, throw it away, or take it to the cemetery and read it to him. The important thing is that you deal with these emotional issues for the good it will do you."

The same applies whether your father is in prison, works long hours or in a faraway country, died before you were even born, or was divorced or kicked out of the home. You name it.

Let's revisit the story of my client, Don, on this point.

"Every time my dad and I get together, any minor thing explodes into an argument. I've tried talking to him in ways you've suggested and we both get defensive, hot-headed, and loud. That's what we do. Every time. He still treats me like a kid thinking he knows better and has to be right. I can never do anything good enough for him. I end up stomping out and slamming the door. I seriously think it's too late. He's beyond changing. I don't even want to try anymore."

"Don, do you remember how you were able to see that your relationship with your dad was at the core of your business failures and divorces?"

"Yes," he said begrudgingly.

"It's important to remember that you are focusing on the conflict rather than on your choices, your relationship, and your personal fulfillment in life.

"Your constant fighting is hiding all that really matters. It's never too late to work on the two of you, but perhaps by focusing on your own needs, it will give you the drive you need to pursue both purposes—your future and your relationship."

It is so easy for us to put up with all the negatives in our lives because we don't want to deal with the conflict. Perhaps the real reason is that we don't know how. We have never learned the tools for dealing with conflict.

Don himself is not a father, so we did not get into future generational issues, but we will cover those as we go. In a later chapter, we'll delve into the details of how Don took the step-by-step, often painful process of reconciliation with his father. The point is, it wasn't too late for them, and isn't for you either.

Fathering in Many Forms

In today's world, lifestyles have changed drastically: we now have divorced parents, single parents, same-sex parents, and alternative and blended family structures, as well as external demands such as racial bias, changing welfare rules, and various societal pressures from advertising, money, culture, and changing value systems added to the mix.

I'm not advocating for or lamenting any of these changes here, simply stating a fact. The point is, the changes make the issue of present and involved fathering more difficult and rare, the negative outcomes of its absence that much more evident.

Even the courts are doing their best, as noted by the US Department of Health and Human Services: "Over the past decade, an interest in fathers and their contributions to family stability and children's healthy development has heightened the attention paid within the child welfare field to identifying, locating and involving fathers."[2] As a result, single father households rose from 500,000 (1 percent) in 1950 to 2.5 million (4 percent) in 2016.[3]

Often a biological father is not present, but given the impact of the male father figure, we have learned that a trusted male father figure or two in the lives of boys and girls can fulfill many of the same fatherly benefits.

Author Stu Weber states, "True fathering has very little to do with biology, but everything to do with responsibly caring for others."[4] For many families, the key defining factor of a father is not who the man is but how he interacts with his children. He may be a grandfather, uncle, older brother, or stepfather. After all, children often identify their father as the man who provides one or all of the following: love, time, education, safety, and material needs.

It is the *role* of the father that is so significant.

Therefore, if the biological father is not available or performing his role, finding the right man or men to fill the void will be worth the effort.

From all this research, we can intuitively conclude one of the single most important tasks of a man's life is learning to be a father. Even when fathers do not share a home with their children, their active involvement can have a lasting and positive impact.

But the past does not have to dictate the future—we can intervene at any time and make a positive impact. We have each known a man about whom we say, "He's a really good father." Such men are good role models. They prove the research. Give attention to them, learn from them. The future of your children, your work, and your personal well-being depends on it.

To quote Stu Weber again, "Whether a man has biological children or not, he is to be applying himself to fathering functions."[5]

The silver lining in all of this is that there are plenty of fathers who are required to be physically absent (for all the reasons we cited before) but are determined to be actively involved in the lives of their children and spouses anyway. They choose to find creative alternatives. These physically absent men are not absent from involvement—rather, they are actively involved, demonstrating powerful father *presence*. This is a great time to remember the story of the two boys from Ukraine in chapter 4.

Although fully-present fathering—when the father is physically and actively involved—is ideal, it is not required for the benefits of presence to have an impact. Being actively involved meets a child's needs in a way that makes a big difference, because what they need is a father who is in a relationship with them.

Whatever the reason for a father not living full-time with his children, there is always a way to be in relationship. Even a deceased father leaves a legacy of influence, one that continues his passivity and negativity or can be so positive it continues in a powerful vibrant way, perhaps for generations.

So far, we've explored the observable impact of fathers across society. If every father were present and engaged with his family, our society would flourish at such a dazzling level we can scarcely imagine it. Though this is far from the reality we face today, we have hope.

In order to actively engage solutions, we must first understand how the negative impact of father absence forms, how it takes root, and how it spreads to every corner of society.

Our journey begins at the foundations of the individual: the development of identity.

Part II

The Cycle of Uninvolvement

Section 1

Father Uninvolvement
Affects the Individual

Chapter 7

Origins of Identity

"Like father like son."

—ANONYMOUS

"If you know the father, you know the son."

—ANONYMOUS

"You are my son, and I am very proud of you."

—GOD TO HIS SON, JESUS

Recently, my wife, Kay, and I were at the Kennedy Space Center in Florida. We stayed after dark to watch a rocket launch. An orange moon, the destination of the ship, was on the rise behind the launch pad. The flash of fire and roaring rumble of ignition was thrilling, even from miles away. We were told the sound is so loud that a load of water is simultaneously dumped from a tower next to the launch pad to help smother the noise and vibration. A person standing too close, even the distance of a football field away, would be killed instantly from the vibration alone. A powerful testament to how a moment can travel across a great distance and still make a serious impact.

This truth can be observed every day in our ordinary lives.

Throughout the Visitor's Center, reference was made to one of the prime motivations for space exploration: the search for our origins. *Where did we come from? What's the meaning of life itself? Who are we? Who am I?* These are questions every human asks themselves at one time or another.

But what factors contribute to the answers?

As soon as we are born, we begin observing our surroundings and learning to fit in. We adapt to our biological needs and to the culture into which we are born, specifically that of our immediate significant influences: family and friends.[1] Our sense of self develops from the norms and values of these cultures. Do we match, fit in, measure up? Or not?

Think about the children in your home versus those next door versus those on the other side of the world. Different cultures have different norms and values that have a unique impact on the children being raised in it and contribute to the unique identity they develop.

Think about looking at yourself in the mirror. What do you see? As a youth, I was fair-skinned and wished I could turn some color from the sun other than red. My hair would never cooperate, and if I could only be a few inches taller...Everything from how we look to how we talk to how we move affects our identity. But no two identities are completely alike, not even identical twins.

Yet how we relate to and are accepted by others is very important in the identity we develop. Raise your hand if you were usually chosen last on the playground. It is this offer of acceptance and belonging that often compels individuals to become members of street gangs— a powerful factor they didn't experience anywhere else.

Things like birth order, personality types, even what we are called is a factor in identity. Names matter. It may be our given name, a positive or negative nickname, or merely an adjective like smart or dumb, handsome or ugly. People tend to play out a self-fulfilling prophecy when it comes to names, becoming what their name means or the adjectives that people assign, becoming what others think of them. Parents beware! I know parents who told their kids they wish they (the kids) had never been born. Imagine the lasting impact of those words from the people who are supposed to love and cherish you most.

The Role of the Parents

The role of the parents is the most influential of all relationships in forming an individual's identity. And it is this identity that will lead to their impact on society. Researchers Oberuč and Zapletal discovered,

> The quality of life of any society is directly dependent
> on the quality of family life.

Both parents play a unique and essential role to the child, as does their relationship to each other. Their findings continue:

> Fulfilling of the functions of the family directly depends on the relationship between the spouses, which is reflected in the relationship between parents and children.

Take a look at the parent-child examples around you. What do their relationships tell you about the husband-wife relationship? From the same study, Oberuč and Zapletal conclude:

> A cold or even hostile, or a completely ruined relationship between spouses does not provide the right conditions for the child's emotional development. A family is therefore a unit, in which the mutual relationships of all its members are important...A woman—mother—has a role that can never be replaced by men, while men have roles that cannot be replaced by anyone else. A man and a woman, as a father and a mother, need each other and complement each other, thus form a whole. Therefore, it is important that the family is complete and that there are both parents present as people whom the child needs.[2]

The next time you are out in a park, notice parents and their children. I remember an instance years ago when I saw a mom and toddler walk up to a retaining wall with a natural stair-step structure. The child pulled away and ran to the steps and started to climb. All kids want to climb. Mom quickly took the child's hand and pulled her away from the steps saying, "No, you're not supposed to climb on those. I don't want you to get hurt." Later, I saw the same toddler with dad. Dad swooped her up and put her on top. "Hey, look at you, Queen of the Castle. You're so good at climbing."

From this context, it's interesting to note that fathers tend to hold their babies and infants as if carrying a football, looking forward with him to wherever they are going and to whatever is coming. Mothers, on the other hand, tend to carry them turned into themselves or looking over their shoulder, seeing where they have already been.

This difference is in how fathers and mothers tend to see the world. Moms often focus on nurturing and protecting, while dads are more likely to expose their kids to all the sights, experiences, and risks that he can. Man's natural approach to life is an attitude of adventure and discovery. He wants to share this with his children, so his basic goal is to pull them out of the nest to prepare them for the world. This is not contrary to mom, and by working together they each present a different approach.

The differences are intended to create a balance rather than a conflict, but we can often tell by observation that it does create some conflict, especially when the parents do not recognize both approaches as necessary. My explanations are an attempt to show how this is true, and to take advantage of the truth rather than to sound as if one is better than the other. It is not to let them turn into conflict, or to suggest that there aren't any variances outside of these scenarios.

Since the roles of mother and father are so essential and different in developing the identity of the child, let's look into them more deeply. After years of studying and observing these roles, certain characteristics have emerged as consistent. It is important to say first that I believe both roles are essential. As mentioned, while there can be overlap and interchange, they are also quite different.

The Role of the Mother

For many generations, perhaps for all of history, mothers have been the solidifying force of the family by nurturing and contributing emotional security during the early years of the child's life. This includes displaying tenderness and providing safety. The basic focus of the mother is on what we call nurture and nesting. Obviously this does not apply to every woman, but it does tend to be inherent when the woman becomes a mother.

One overarching characteristic of the mother is unconditional love. She loves her children through all their shortcomings of looks, abilities, or talents. Their relationship builds an emotional strength that will help the child find their place in society.

Psychological research shows that the relationship with one's mother has the most influence on how we imagine, trust, and relate to God.[3] This is an area of identity development that is probably assumed more than it is realized. Again, from researchers Oberuc and Zapletal:

> ...It is very important that the child receives as many pleasant inputs at an early age (caress, smile, and understanding) as possible. It is known that the shortage of these is reflected in latter aggression or inaccurate adaptation of a young person to social regulations. Experts agree that children who could not grow up in the care of their mother, especially at pre-school age, when the emotional development is the most intense, are disadvantaged.[4]

While written in the negative, this statement emphasizes the significance of the nurturing and nesting roles of the mother. As mentioned already, not every mother fits this mold.

The Role of the Father

Equally as important as the mother in the development of a child's identity is the father. Once again, this is not a competition or even a comparison. It is a description of each parent's role.

Research from all sources I found repeatedly says that nothing is more important to a young man, or a young woman, than a father's love, respect, and acceptance. These attributes are demonstrated through his words and actions—for better or worse, he is a role model. Before he lets things get in the way to tarnish his image, everyone in the family, including his wife, naturally looks to him to be the leader and the hero, to offer protection, identity, and affirmation.

In chapter 3, we described the four influences of a father including physical, emotional, psychological, and spiritual. They each fit under the concept of *protection,* with the image of dad being a barrier against negative influences that may cause fear and damage to the family. It also gives the image of building truth, wisdom, and strength so children develop their own ability to withstand the negative influences that will come. Also inherent in the word protection is provision: the father provides for his family to protect them with the basic needs of life and then some.

Provision is typically the reason either one or both parents go to work. It is also a way to fulfill our purpose, skills, and abilities, but I believe we would find other ways to be fulfilled if the basic need to provide didn't exist. I bring this up because so often the father (or the mother) goes to work or decides to start a family business with the original motivation to provide. But soon the focus changes from being a successful provider to being a successful worker. The emphasis on protecting the physical, emotional, psychological, and spiritual aspects of each member of the family shifts to protecting one's status and success on the job at the expense of protecting the family or even spending time with them. Work does take a lot of time, effort, and focus, but at what cost to our families? How often do we intentionally balance the time or energy we spend at work with the protection and provision needs of our family members?

Identity and Affirmation for Sons

Identity comes from all the influences that surround us. Those influences tell us who we are, whose we are and how we fit into the life around us. As important as this is, we need to hear the answers from the strongest influences, our parents. Studies show that both sons and daughters look primarily to their father to discover their own identity. They are waiting to hear what dad has to say and to show them his love.

His *unconditional love.*

Growing up, boys have powerful desires to prove themselves and have adventures. These desires prompt some basic emotional questions. *Who am I? Do I have what it takes? To be strong? To be wise? To be respected? Do I have what it takes to be a man?*

Boys don't consciously realize they're asking these questions, but they are. In fact, boys are wondering about them from the time they are four or five years old. These questions repeat for life.

Fathers and father figures are designed to be the ones to answer.

In his captivating book, *Wild at Heart,* John Eldredge says,

> A boy learns who he is and what he's got from a man, or a company of men. He cannot learn it any other place. He cannot learn it from other boys, and he cannot learn it from the world of women. The plan from the beginning of time was that his father would lay the foundation for a young boy's heart, and pass on to him that essential knowledge and confidence in his strength.[5]

This "passing on" is done through modeling, instruction, and affirmations. The father sees his son behave, speak, or accomplish things that are worthy of notice—and he notices! He lets his son know that he approves in ways that accumulate into an identity.

The lack of affirmation has a similar yet opposite effect. Either way, the son will come to believe in the identity of himself that is affirmed or denied.

It becomes a self-fulfilling prophecy.

We get a glimpse of a child's emotional needs by watching them play. Most boys gravitate to fighting battles and winning, or having great adventure where daring, bravery, and strength are needed to prove themselves. They demonstrate being strong even if they aren't strong. They desire to be powerful because that's how they see themselves—the hero! This is also the vision they have of their father, that he is strong and brave. They want to be like him.

This vision fades in the teen years as the boy begins to see that his father is not really the hero he thought he was. This demonstrates the need for an even stronger bond so dad can help his son as he grows to move on to become a man. The wise father allows the son's passion for adventure and proving himself to become a basis for living a life of integrity and contribution.

Identity and Affirmation for Daughters

The seemingly incongruous reality is that girls also find their identity primarily through their fathers. A girl's identity is crafted from the same methods as a boy's—by being noticed, valued, and affirmed. The influence of fathers on girls carries well into adulthood.

How a girl is treated by her father as she is growing up helps shape her view of men in general and what she expects from them. It sets a standard. Further, the relationship she had with her dad growing up will be reflected in how girls relate to men while dating and in marriage. A well-known adage says girls end up marrying men like their fathers. It contains a lot of truth.

Dr. Meg Meeker, pediatrician and author, painted this powerful reality when she said:

> Fathers, more than anyone else, set the course for a daughter's life. And I have watched daughters talk to fathers. When you come in the room, they change. Everything about them changes: their eyes, their mouths, their gestures, their body language. Daughters are never lukewarm in the presence of their fathers.
>
> They might take their mothers for granted, but not you. They light up—or they cry. They watch you intensely. They hang on your words. They hope for your attention, and they wait for it in frustration—or in despair. They need a gesture of approval, a nod of encouragement, or even simple eye contact to let them know you care and are willing to help.
>
> When she's in your company, your daughter tries harder to excel. When you teach her, she learns more rapidly. When you guide her, she gains confidence. If you fully understood just how profoundly you can influence your daughter's life, you would be overwhelmed.[6]

Girls so desperately want their father's attention and affirmation that they will watch his eyes to see what matters to him. They watch to see how he looks at other women, what he notices, which women he notices with admiration, and which ones he turns his nose at.

This man, this hero in their lives, this one they look to for their very identity, determines what matters to him by what he is looking at. And then the daughters strive to match what gains his attention. If he looks admiringly at slender women, they will work to be slender, maybe too slender.

This is so striking that a study was done that showed anorexia and bulimia can most often be traced back to girls' perceptions of their fathers.

Psychologist John Toussaint says, "Fathers play an important role in the development of eating disorders, self-esteem and body satisfaction." He also found a link between parental rejection and women developing bulimia. This isn't always cause and effect, but "dysfunctional families and stress are certainly factors in the development of eating disorders."[7]

As was pointed out with boys, girls are also prompted to ask basic emotional questions. Theirs include "Who am I? Do I have character? Am I lovely, desirable, respected? Do I have what it takes to be a woman?"

Once again, fathers are designed to be the one to answer these questions Psychotherapist and author Dr. Mary Jo Rapini says:

> We know that children do better with involved fathers than without. That goes for both boys and girls. We also know that a teenage girl's sexual behavior tends to be more responsible if she has a present, involved dad...fathers who pay attention to their daughters' achievements, interests, and characters tend to produce confident adults, whereas fathers who dwell on their daughters' appearance tend to damage their self-esteem. A girl who grows up without a father tends to have a poorer self image than those with fathers who are active in their upbringing...Studies show that dads give girls 90 percent of their self-esteem before the age of twelve.[8]

Back to the playground to watch how girls play: concerning the emotional needs for affirmation, girls also want adventure, but the focus is not on the adventure but rather on the relationship—someone with whom to share the adventure.

In *Wild at Heart,* Eldridge goes on to say when it comes to the battle the boys are fighting on the playground, girls want to be fought for, to be wanted.[9] This is merely another form of the affirmation a girl seeks from her father, the affirmation that she has a unique inner beauty to reveal and that others will be delighted in her. Along with their father, girls seek to gain this delight from others during play.

The Power of a Father

All humanity seems to crave identity. We want to know who we are and why we are here, as individuals and as the collective of humanity. But the real source of our personal identity is right here: our fathers.

Many will wonder how that can be. But I believe we all know deep within that it is true. That the father is designed to be the one who gives us our identity. Most of us are just too messed up with too much relational baggage for it to work that way, and so we conclude it doesn't.

Our father's presence is required for the balance of life as we desire it—as we want it, hope for it, require it.

But what happens when our father's influence builds a negative identity instead of a positive one?

Chapter 8

The Father Wound

"Dad failed me.

Dad owns every bit of those failures.

But there was more to see.

Dad lived fatherless, too.

I have to let him go free."

−DAVID L ELLIS, AUTHOR,

LOSING DAD, FINDING FATHER

As noted in the previous chapter, identity comes primarily through the father along with other factors of the environment—and in both cases, by what is and what isn't there.

Absence is defined as the state of being away from a place or person. From a child's perspective, father absence feels more like abandonment. Abandonment means to *"give up* or discontinue any further interest in something because of discouragement, weariness, or distaste."[1] When a person is abandoned, they have been physically left behind, with no remaining contact or recourse for help.

This act of abandonment creates a wound, one that is swift and deep. If the absence is due to a father's death, the nature of the wound may be different, but there are very often still abandonment issues to work through.

When a father dies, there is no choice in the matter as there is for all other reasons of absence. So while a father's death can be excruciatingly painful for a child, it is not as difficult as having an absent father. This is simply because, as far as a child is concerned, the father's absence is a result of choice. Whatever that choice was, it resulted either directly or indirectly in giving up time with the child for something else, and the child knows he or she is not being chosen. Authors Roland Warren and Gordon Dalbey respectively describe the father wound as follows:

> Kids have a hole in their soul in the shape of their dad. And if a father is unwilling or unable to fill that hole, it can leave a *wound* that is not easily healed.[2]

> The father-wound is *a wound of absence*. Therefore, it's harder to recognize than other wounds—and ultimately, more destructive.[3]

This wound is so devastating that it is the foundation of the many stories of youth who become defiant about not needing their father: he is dead to them. It's not a matter of *just getting over it*.

In DadsFirst, we work with groups of men to heal from these wounds. In one session, the topic was abandonment. Men are not known for making wise decisions about their own lives that may influence—and abandon—their children, but their years of raw experience give them a certain insight that draws listeners in.

As we talked about being abandoned, one tough old bird shared a thoughtful epiphany. "Your father is the first person in your life who will choose you, or not."

The fellow next to him chimed in, "When your father's not there, when he doesn't choose you, it's like the floor falls out and there is no bottom."

A third man said, "At that point, you have two choices. You can respond with hatred and buy into all the repercussions that create a negative life, or you can choose to forgive and find your way."

It was a powerful moment to witness because we could see the previous lessons taking root in these men as they reflected on their lives and made it their own.

Repercussions of the Wound

Author Dan Allender describes the history of the ancient Near East, saying, "If a boy's father died, he lost his place, his name, and his inheritance. He became an orphan—a boy without *protection*, without *provision*, and without an *identity*."[4]

A father helps his son understand his masculinity and helps his daughter understand her femininity. Without this assistance, the son has no clear goal to shoot for, no idea of what masculinity looks like for himself.

The average man today has learned well from his mother to embrace his *feminine side* and become tender and receptive—which is a great gift—but because his father has been emotionally and often physically absent, he hasn't learned to embrace his more deliberate *masculine side*. His identity is not fully rounded.

Poet and author Robert Bly declared that, without a father to secure him in his masculine identity, the man abdicates his destiny and looks to the woman, as mom, to define his nature and purpose. Ultimately, therefore, he embraces a false femininity and becomes passive.[5] Instead of modeling masculinity, an absent father models abandonment. The son really wants to be like his father, but the comparison between masculinity and abandonment, as Gordon Dalbey says, "fills him with shame."[6]

Author Randy Hix explains, "As a result of a father's absence, sons... obsessed with being 'man enough,' become philanderers, controllers, and competitors—constantly overcompensating for their loss of a true role model, [and] sorely unprepared for family life. This...also affects the way young men relate to the opposite sex and women in general."[7]

A daughter, too, without a father's guidance, approaches men in her life without understanding who or what they are, what she should expect from them, or how to develop mutual trust and respect. She misses his model of how to give and receive affection and tenderness.

Unfortunately, even fathers who are present and wonderful fathers and husbands, often do not understand his role in imparting masculinity and femininity to his children.

Attempting to Fill the Void

Dan Allender explains how our response turns against our absent father: "There are many ways of becoming an orphan, but they all lead to the same end: a swirl of desire to touch our absent father's face and hear him speak our name. The desire is more than most of us can bear, and we turn against that ache by killing all our desire to feel safe in our father's presence."[8]

Our inner drive and need for identity is so strong that, if we don't get it through the influence of our father or a good father figure, we will continue to look for it in other ways. Those ways have been identified and grouped into five categories by author Ken Canfield: drugs and alcohol, sexual activity, money and possessions, accolades and achievement, and being accepted.[9]

Drugs and alcohol. There are many causes of addictions, but at the core of them all is this struggle with identity. Identity is our source of strength and direction for life, and yet it scares the life out of us. Finding and owning it means we have to show up. We have to be real and take on the power inherent in that identity.

Author John Eldredge makes the statement that our addictions are a result of running from our strengths.[10] Our addictions become a way to hide from ourselves. We may fear we can't measure up, or we don't want to accept the responsibility. This interesting paradox indicates that we struggle so hard to find our identity that, when we begin to find it, we may be so impacted by it that we push it away, more afraid of our strengths than our weaknesses.

Sexual activity. As explained in chapter 7, girls learn that they are lovely, desirable, and have what it takes to be a woman from their father. If he is not available to help them discover this area of identity, they will look to discover this important value on their own. For instance, a girl may assume that if she gives her body to a man, it will show she is lovely and desirable. Or a boy may attempt to prove his masculinity by "conquering" a girl. Neither act is capable of determining the purpose of the search—finding one's identity and worth. Neither one will give that kind of affirmation.

Money and possessions. This assumes that possessing things proves worth and identity. As an example, a young man may think if he has a smoking hot sports car it will show others that he is a person who knows who he is—self-confident, "in the know," wild. I love hot cars, and there are good reasons to have them, but they are inanimate objects, incapable of proving worth and identity.

Every spring, local newspapers will run photos of graduating high school seniors with short blurbs about their future plans and goals. For the young men, overwhelmingly it is all about money, how they can make the most, or which degree or job will make them the most. There seems to be an unwritten agreement that money will buy identity, self-worth, and success in life. But those who have unspeakable wealth will be the first to tell you there is never enough.

Accolades and Achievement. As parents, we often promote achievement through such actions as paying our children for getting good grades. Now I believe that can be done appropriately as a way to reward achievement. However, we can also look around and see many people who obviously are attempting to get their sense of value, confidence, worth, and identity through their achievement or by being successful. Achievement may be praiseworthy, and one may even receive affirmations, but it raises questions of one's values and motives when using it as a means of knowing who they are.

Belonging and/or being accepted. This lies at the core of identity and is the root and motivation for the other four, which essentially are all attempts to be accepted. We all know how good it feels to be accepted by friends or to be chosen for a team. If we feel we belong, we take on the identity of the group (family, club, team), which gives us a sense of who we are.

Perhaps the best example of the misplaced sense of belonging comes from street gangs. While gangs provide family-type acceptance, they can only offer a false sense of true identity. George Knox, a gang researcher, says, "The fact that kids stay in gangs indicates that their families are failing to instill in them the notion that they belong, that they deserve better." He says, "The deeper a kid's involvement in a gang, the more dysfunctional his/her family life."[11]

Tom Schneider, a probation officer in Chicago adds, "Most of the young gang members I've worked with don't have adequate fathers or male role models."[12]

Fathers are crucial to combating the negative issues of sexual activity, profanity, pornography, gambling, lying, alcohol, and drug use. I have addressed the father influence in these areas and have found it has been well documented in over 22,000 separate sets of data and a review of twenty-four empirical studies.

Sons need to see what real masculinity is from their fathers, but instead many dads today are caught in the world of addictions—be it work or sports, drugs or pornography, even religious legalism—all masks that hide their real identity, hideouts that intentionally or inadvertently keep them from showing up at home.

Stu Weber states, "Another meaning for fatherlessness is a lack of manhood, for the term *father* is the consummate masculine word. A present father is applied masculinity at its best. True fathering has...everything to do with responsibly caring for others...but men in America today seem to be looking out more for themselves than others."[13]

When we don't get the questions of identity answered at home, we go elsewhere and typically get the wrong answers that leave us unfulfilled. The search for identity will continue into adult life and old age, and will remain unanswered and unfulfilled even in death—*unless* there is a positive intervention that helps a person find the truth they are missing.

Generating a Negative Identity

When I was growing up, my father had his own business—not really a family business, but he was self-employed. That in itself took some guts to put himself out there like that, and he was successful enough to provide a good middle class living. To make it possible, he was gone a lot. We ate supper later in the evening to allow him to work a long day and still make it to the table. We did things as a family, but rarely one-on-one with dad. We didn't do fun or adventurous things, like fishing, camping, or going to Cubs games. We didn't even play catch. I was lucky enough to have uncles who engaged with me this way. They stepped in and fulfilled some of the father roles for my dad, but they were only temporary role models.

As a kid, I was always trying to make things out of wood, everything from birdhouses to makeshift scooters to forts. My dad was great with tools, but as I remember it, he never showed me how to use them or helped me build anything. In fact, sometimes when he would see my end result—the bent nails, chewed-up saw cuts, the pile of wood thrown against the wall in anger—he'd chuckle. I saw and felt him laughing at me. I also saw that my responses of anger mimicked his responses. I was learning the wrong things.

One of the roles of parents is to *interpret life's experiences for the kids*, not ridicule their attempts. Kids come to all kinds of silly or wrong conclusions based on how things go and what they are told. As a kid, I was frustrated with the stupid birdhouse, got angry, and smashed it to pieces. My response was two-fold: 1) I made a negative agreement[14] with and about myself that I did not have the ability to do that kind of work, and 2) I developed the unhealthy idea that everything I tried to do I would have to do on my own. If it came out good, I could be proud. If it came out bad, no one would ever know. That attitude followed me my whole life.

I still look back in those days wondering, "Dad, where were you? Why didn't you help me? Why didn't you put your arm around me and reassure me I was okay? To tell me I had what it takes to be your son and to grow with confidence and maturity? I needed you, I wanted you, but you weren't there." I often wondered if he was embarrassed by me.

My dad was absent emotionally and psychologically, and I felt and lived with the consequences from then on.

I had been a good student up through fifth grade. Then we moved, and my world came crashing down. I lost some of my friends, my neighborhood, my school, everything that was a part of my identity. In addition, there was no understanding or intervention from my folks as to my pain and struggle with my sense of loss. From then through high school, my grades plummeted. I didn't care about school because no one else seemed to care. My sense of abandonment grew. I needed help but no one heard me. They only assumed I was not a scholar. Even in high school, I was given a blank diploma at graduation because of the tests and work I still had to complete.

Somehow I made it into college, by the skin of my teeth, on a probationary basis depending on getting my grades up. Apparently, someone saw potential in me. Gradually my grades did improve, and I graduated to become—of all things—a teacher. I started with high school but for many years taught middle school as well. I had a knack for finding those kids who just moved in to the school district and were timid, afraid, lost, and quite obviously abandoned. I knew what they were going through and stopped to listen. As hard as it was for me to go through as a boy, there apparently was a future purpose for someone else's benefit. I found myself filling part of a father's role for these students, helping them interpret their experiences in a different, more positive light.

But in terms of relationships, values, identity, dating, money, and life management, I was still on my own. As a music major in college, I recall my supervisor working with me on playing a piece of music on my horn. As he worked to get me to put more of myself into it, to express some energy and expression, he said, "You're playing like you are *tim*-id, Tim."

That comment was a defining moment for me in two ways. First, it was a rare expression of someone reaching inside of me and pulling out an ugly trait that I needed to look at. It was a trait that I hated, and another person finally took the risk to point it out. This was a rare experience for me, and unfortunately, I imagine it is rare for most people.

I always struggled to do and learn without adequate training, wisdom, and guidance, rarely asking for help or not realizing I could. This was true in my teaching, my family life, my remodeling business, and all the other occupations I have talked about already. My internal message was that others (dad) are not available to give the help I need and want. Or worse yet, they don't see me as worthy of their attention and haven't chosen me. I learned early that I had to figure life out on my own, so I rarely asked and was rarely told. In looking back, I always wished I had a mentor. I wish with all my heart that mentor had been my dad.

Second, in looking back from later years, I realized that was a part of the passivity from my father that took several decades to intentionally phase out of my identity and to keep it from affecting my own children's lives.

In recent years, as I have been studying the role of the father, I know now that was his job—to come alongside, to listen, to try to understand, to empathize, to mentor, instruct, guide, interpret all those crazy experiences of life for me, to prepare me for the world. He didn't. He abandoned me.

I have also learned he didn't avoid me on purpose. He was only being the father he had observed from his father. That doesn't lessen my pain, but it brings understanding along with grace, forgiveness, and reconciliation. And that is what lessens the pain.

Today, I identify timidity as the *lack of confidence*. That trait still haunts me in subtle ways. Anyone who knows me, well or not, describes me as a confident person. That's not because of a veneer or mask that I have mastered, but it is a real and strong reality. I have come to know my identity with passion, self-confidence, and truth—it is who I am. However, on occasion, it flees from me and I revert back to the passive *tim*-idity of my youth. The old tapes start playing and I hear the familiar lies like a whisper in my ear: "You never could build a birdhouse, fit into a crowd, or perform with confidence."

How can a wise father help to interpret life for his children? First of all, he could see what his son is doing and ask if he wants help. Regardless of giving help, he must give affirmation: "Son, good job. I can see with some practice and instruction that you will be good at working with your hands. Would you like me to help you learn and practice?" He might also see that his son won't be good at certain activities and guide him into areas for which he has natural abilities, affirming him as he goes.

Once I became aware of this concept, I wondered, who would I have become if my father had not been a passive man? Who would I have become if I'd not had to first overcome the passivity I learned from my father?

These same questions apply to the millions of passive men out there, hiding, afraid to show up, afraid to be the men they were intended to be. Think of the impact asking these questions could have. Think of the millions of children, also dutifully learning how to be passive, to hide, to be afraid of becoming who they were destined to be. What would our world be like if our collective father wounds were healed?

Chapter 9

The Father Influence in Action

"If we do not intentionally deal with what has impacted
us, we will most assuredly repeat the same thing."
—RICHARD ROHR, AUTHOR

Both parents teach by example and words how to perceive and evaluate right from wrong, how to relate to others, and how to decide for themselves.

An essential lesson for every father is seeing that, present or absent, he is the primary influencer for good or bad in the lives of those around him.

Owning Your Influence

We change ourselves and others not by changing our behavior but by first changing how we see others. We get into trouble because we tend to see others as objects, not as individuals.

When this first hit home for me, I was in the business of teaching students, but I was the one doing the learning. I used to get so upset with kids who were misbehaving (or I assumed they were misbehaving) and it would trigger my temper, a generational trait I picked up from my father. When they acted out—or appeared to—I immediately put them in a box of those who had no respect, were immature, had no goals, held few values or ideals, must have come from undisciplined homes, and so on. You get the picture.

In essence, I was the one who had no respect for them and did not value them as individuals. I assumed they fit the box that I had pre-designed and saw them more as objects than individual people with hopes, dreams, challenges, trials, and feelings of their own. I also did not consider how I might be contributing to their difficulties, challenges, and negative view of leadership. It was possible that I was neglecting or mistreating them not because of who they were but because of the imaginary box in which I had put them. Even the box was likely to be misconceived because it existed primarily to justify my own behavior and thinking.

This is important to consider as we look at the father role in the family, in business, and any other walk or activity in life. From the premise presented so far, we see the father role as the key factor in the lives of his children from birth to death. From the pressure of being a dad in any setting, it can be easy for him to shut out his kids and wife from important activity at all levels. We also learned that dad is (as is each of us) pressured by the need to be right. The need to be right is also affected by what we perceive to be right. To be right, he will blame and accuse others to shift blame from himself—and some of this will be very subtle. He may get impatient and frustrated with them purely due to the boxes he has assigned to them.

"Don't slam the screen door!" A dad yells as his young kids run out the door. *Wham!* the door hits home again. He hates that loud bang, but so far his only solution has been to yell.

Why do they have to run out? Why do they have to be so thoughtless? Why can't they be more careful? Don't they remember what I just told them? Dad keeps imagining his kids as more than kids.

A while later, all the kids are playing on the front porch and dad comes out to run an errand. *Wham!* the screen door slams shut. The kids yell as one, "Don't slam the door!"

Dad says, "I tried to catch it. My arms were full. Why didn't someone help me?"

From dad's perspective, he can have an excuse for slamming the door but no one else can. In fact, his error becomes their fault.

We tend to do this with everyone around us in our lives, whether employees, customers, young children, teenage children, adult children, spouses, senior family members, those sick or handicapped, people from other races or cultures, and the list goes on. What we perceive to be right is usually a very narrow and prejudiced view. As you read this, memories likely came to mind of you or others caught in similar settings. That helps in understanding this concept.

Operating in Self-Deception

The reality is that dad (or any one of us) is also operating from his own box. It's a box called self-deception. Self-deception is the problem of not knowing, and resisting the possibility, that one has a problem.[1] We deceive ourselves into thinking we are okay and everyone else has a messed up sense of priorities, values, and ideas.

Let's go back to my story as a teacher and seeing misbehaving students as being in a box. The reality is that I was seeing them from my own box. I had justified myself into thinking the problem was all theirs and I was okay. One day, when the other teachers and I were getting mad about test results and student behavior, a mentor said something that sticks with me to this day. He silenced all of us when he said, "If a kid isn't doing something right, it's because we haven't taught him the right way to do it."

I think we all hated the idea that it was our fault instead of the kids', but he was right! This would never be resolved as long as I had myself in this box.

Later, as I contemplated this dilemma, a thought came to me like a lightning bolt: *Jesus loves those kids at least as much as he loves me.* In his sight, we are the same. Those words broke me on the spot. I began seeing the kids as having value and self-worth—individuals with the same needs and desires for love and acceptance as I had. That realization not only took me out of my own box, but it also took away the false box I had designed for them. It was a great learning and life-shaping moment for me—and for the relationships I had with students. I was amazed at how much the kids had changed, but of course, I had changed, not them. And it wasn't my behavior that changed, it was my way of seeing them. For an example of this way of seeing, watch the "there is no spoon" scene from the film *The Matrix*.

Self-deception is also called self-betrayal. As we see others in a way that puts them in a box, it hurts us more than it hurts them. It betrays everything we do and how we view ourselves.

The authors of *Leadership and Self-Deception* list six factors that *don't* work when we are in our own box.[2] They are:

1. Trying to change others

2. Doing my best to "cope" with others

3. Leaving

4. Communicating

5. Implementing new skills or techniques

6. Changing my own behavior

Each of these factors hits fathers and business owners (and teachers) square in the face. We try to bring about change through these six ways that don't work. Think about each one and how you have attempted to implement it for change. We can't even do number six: bring about change by changing our own behavior.[3]

Mentoring Their Belief Systems

Many parents don't want to influence their child's value and belief systems—they want the child to develop and choose on their own. I'm all for allowing kids great freedom in discovering who they are, but if we don't provide them with some direction and a value system, someone else will—and it will likely differ from ours, toward one we're not too happy about.

If you leave it up to children to find their own value and belief system, don't be surprised by who they become. Whether or not parents want to have an influence, they do. At least be intentional about it.

The idea that we ought to let kids discover their own moral, emotional, physical, and spiritual codes without informed guidance is like being in a boat without a rudder. It naively assumes they will pursue their own codes for life with wise investigation and evaluation before they even reach an age of maturity that allows for such activity. The reality is far from that. They are open to following whatever breeze that comes along to catch their fancy.

What I have observed in similar cases is that the child grows up with no center, with no strong system that says, "This is who I am, and this is what I believe." This, in turn, often results in situational ethics: whatever is good for the given situation is good enough for me.

In such a so-called value system, there is no right or wrong, truth or lie, or boundaries to live by, either individually or corporately. Interestingly, this is a form of anarchy favoring individual rule, which also breeds entitlement. "Don't tell me what to do, but give me everything I want—*now.*"

With the father gone from so many families and business settings in today's society, the moral compass is missing for young people. Due to this lack of leadership, they end up creating their own moral code based on convenience, feelings, and selfishness. This, in turn, informs and dictates our behavior towards them, and the moral compass shifts a bit more. We wonder what's wrong with them and why they can't be "like us" until we finally take a hard look at our own role, behavior, and values.

Of course, it is nothing new. As each generation is left to their own conclusions, they are more likely to distance themselves from the parenting style of their parents in an increasingly impacting way. And yet, as we will see, even in this distancing, adult children still unconsciously repeat so many patterns of their parents. It just comes out differently.

Beware the Teaching of Bias

When I was a young teenager, I recall driving in my home city of Chicago one day with my dad. As we went through a neighborhood of people from another culture, I asked him about an article of clothing the young men were wearing. His response was to say "Oh, they all dress like that." From his tone, it was clear he did not mean it as a compliment.

Years later, I also recall wondering why I seemed to be so biased for or against various groups or individual people. I realized that much of it had come from the influence of both mom and dad, who, of course, had been influenced in that way by their parents, and so on. Many others in society around me had contributed to my prejudice, as well. In reality, most of us grow up in a prejudiced setting.

This bias is an example of putting people in a box and seeing and treating them as objects and not individuals. Everyone around me seemed to see others in boxes of their own making. Society is made up primarily of biased people. It is a key factor in racism, wars, prejudice, fences—and family divides.

On occasion, I began to notice a few people who approached others with an automatic respect, admiration, and an easy welcoming spirit. It surprised me, and I admired them for this ability. Their approach was so freeing and friendly—and so contrary to what I had learned. I'm sure they did categorize others at some point, but for the most part, they did not, and it was refreshing. To live like that towards others is a challenge, and I don't believe it's possible for anyone to escape bias entirely. Are there people in your life that you see for how you judge them rather than for who they are?

To make this a bit more practical, one of my clients told me he saw himself as "hardworking, sensitive, fair, important, and caring." He was the father and founder of his family run business. He also saw himself as a victim when he described how other family members would try to control him—his wife in particular. By contrast, he saw his twenty-something son, who was employed at the business, as lazy, a lousy worker, unwilling to fit the work culture, inappropriate, and completely unlike his older brother.

Does that help in putting appropriate words to how we see ourselves vs. the negative ones we assume for others? What words would you use to describe how you see yourself? Your spouse? Each of your children? Your employees, boss, or co-workers? In each case, do you see them as individuals with feelings, hopes, dreams, needs, and concerns as valid as your own, or not? Do you see the reality of who you are, or do you see yourself through "rose-colored glasses"?

When we put others and ourselves into predetermined boxes, we hide the truth about them and about ourselves. Rather than finding solutions to fix things, we end up interfering with potential solutions. This predetermined mindset shuts out people and their ideas and perspectives.

The Need to Be Right

A study was done a few years ago to try to determine the cause leading up to divorce. When asked what that might be, most say money, sex, communication, infidelity, addictions, or whatever else their experience may have dished up. Interestingly, the results indicate that the reason is true for the breakup of any relationship, not just marriage.

The conclusion of the study was the need to be right—even when we're wrong. It seems as humans that we have this built in need to protect ourselves, our self-esteem, our sense of self-worth, and our identity so profoundly that we will blame and accuse everyone else of our problems rather than take the blame ourselves. Of course, at the root of this need is pride. Also known as ego, pride comes out as extreme selfishness and self-centeredness.

I included the topic in this chapter because it is so subtle and fundamental in terms of the father's influence. Next to understanding the uninvolved father, this may be the most important issue in the book. The father is the masculine role model for good, and having to be right will only destroy identity, self-esteem, and confidence in other family members. In watching tension in other family's dynamics at work, notice that the need to be right will typically be at the root of the tension. It will usually be the father who is demonstrating his need to be right and all the kids will be watching—and learning.

In what ways have you noticed yourself, or others at home or at work demonstrating the need to be right regardless of whether they are or not? Once this tactic is known, it becomes quite evident when it is being used. It is obvious, obnoxious, and obtuse.

Modeling Masculinity

One of the roles of the father is to pass on the masculine role to sons and daughters. At first we might accept that idea as "of course," but then in thinking about it we have to raise the question: What is true masculinity? What ought men to be as masculine beings, and how has the term become misunderstood? Through advertising and other media, we may come to the conclusion that it has to do with being physically big, brave and strong, without expressions of emotion or affection, sexually active, and successful in what he does and earns.

Over many centuries, society as a whole has come to allow a false sense of authority for men masked as power. In most instances, men tend to rule because of being bigger, louder, meaner, or simply by being male and because they are more prominent for one reason or another than other men, rather than because of who they are and what that "being" brings to the table. This kind of power only serves to hurt everyone. Women, children, and less prominent men become subservient and wounded and men who use false power ultimately become weak and ineffective because what they are exerting power about doesn't matter.

In this regard, I am reminded of the Roman Empire and how it ruled with brute force. It was a physical domination that, while it did bring about the development of improved hygiene, architecture, roads, and politics, it was primarily driven and sustained by the might of its army. In describing how the Prophet Jesus related to the Romans and specifically to the Roman Governor, Pontius Pilate, author Richard Rohr says that he "ignored them as the ultimate negation of false power."[4] Jesus evidently understood not only false and true power but false and true masculinity.

True masculinity that fathers are to introduce to their children is based on character qualities such as integrity, equality, servant leadership, a model of love and respect for the mother of his children, truth-telling, honesty, providing and protecting, courage, adventure, emotional expressiveness, involvement, consistency, commitment, spiritual example, and leadership. Now that's masculinity that is attainable by all male human beings. It is quite different and compelling compared to the self-reliant man who may be silent because in reality he is hiding behind a mask or because he is a testosterone driven, physically strong man using his physical strength as a display of false power.

Masculinity is about becoming a man, about understanding one's identity. Shaquille (Shaq) O'Neil, the great 7'1" NBA basketball star from 1992 to 2011, wrote a rap about his step-father, Philip Harrison. Shaq thanks Phil for keeping his responsibility of commitment, owing his success to Phil's discipline, how he raised him to be an entrepreneur, and that he made basketball a priority. Shaq makes it clear that Phil was his true father, because his biological father didn't bother—it was Phil who took him from a boy to a man.[5]

Generational Impact

As we've discussed, fathers are a key component in forming a child's identity, which is a direct result of their presence and absence. And, as we've seen in Don's story, this identity remains with them throughout adulthood.

When these children become adults and, more often than not, go on to be fathers and mothers themselves, they bring with them all that they've learned, and then model it for others. Whether the children duplicate what has been modeled for them or actively take an opposite stance, either way they are living and parenting from this place of influence by their parents.

And so it goes through generations.

This ongoing and recurring influence shapes individuals, these individuals then shape society, and society in turn reflects back to further shape individuals.

We've all been influenced for generations before us, yet we rarely think about it. We may recognize social norms and movements as a whole, but don't often tie them back to individual choices made daily by fathers and mothers.

This is precisely where we find ourselves today, suffering from the same broken models as so many who came before. And yet, this is simultaneously why we have achieved the social progress we have. Society can be changed for the better, but only with intention. More to come on that in Part III.

First, let's look at the patterns of influence that play out in the family unit.

Section 2

The Uninvolved Father
Affects the Family

Chapter 10

Fathers Out of Balance

*"We need fathers to realize that what makes you a man is not
the ability to have a child, it's the courage to raise one."*

— PRESIDENT BARACK OBAMA

My middle-aged son recently had a job crisis that caused him a great deal of angst. He likes to process such things with many people, so he drew associates, friends, and family members into the fray.

At this time, he had four daughters in their twenties. In response to his dilemma, his twenty-three-year-old daughter said to him, "Dad, you are central to what happens in this family. You affect everything that goes on in our lives."

Her wise observation was full of insight, which helped to bring her father to an action step and move beyond analysis paralysis to restore perspective, security, and balance to the family.

Setting the Tone

Fathers set the mood, the agenda, and the attitudes in family and business life. Yes, mothers do as well, but in this book we are focusing on the involved father. What's more, there are aspects that only fathers fulfill.

In reality, my granddaughter's statement can apply to any member of the family as can be seen in these three diagrams.[1] Each circle represents a family member, and each arrow indicates how they are interrelated and interdependent.

Family Interactions

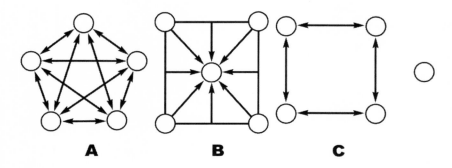

In figure A, each member is connected to every other member who feels and is affected by every other member.

In figure B, one member requires the attention and focus of the others due to physical, emotional, psychological, or spiritual problems. The family has adjusted to give the hurting member the attention they need to recover. This is okay when it is a temporary situation and if the family will readjust back to figure A when it ends. This pattern represented my son's family in his job crisis. Any member of the family can move into the center as needed. This pattern is not okay when it continues beyond the temporary situation.

Figure C represents one member of the family that is essentially absent from the family setting yet is still considered to be part of the family.

In this pattern, the member that is isolated is not a contributing member and is enabled to under-function. The family becomes, in essence, stuck.

While there may be many causes and reasons for the C pattern, it is a good representation of the family of an uninvolved, passive father. While the isolated member may become isolated without having a choice (such as a debilitating illness), when that member is the unengaged father, it is usually a result of his choices (he may choose being at work over being with his family, for example). In that case, the father may be at home much of the time but not a part of the relationships of the rest of the family, as shown by the arrows. As a result, he is not central to the family. He does, however, still influence the tone and character of the family and its members because of the drain he causes on relationships, responsibilities, finances, and time. The visible leadership of the family shifts solely to the mother or even to the kids.

The fallacy of the diagram is that it looks as if the rest of the family is balanced and functional. With the father out of the picture but still influencing it, the children fall under the absent father syndrome, or as VanVonderen points out, the structure actually reverts to diagram B, "because families *are* systems, there really can never be a diagram C."[2]

Gateway to Passivity

Fathers are wired to provide. That's one of the reasons they go to work or start a family business.

This is where the challenge comes in, to evaluate what really matters about going to work. Providing for the family begins as an altruistic goal that soon makes an inevitable turn. The focus soon becomes one of making the business successful and making the father successful in business. The drive for success makes it easy to misplace the original drive: to provide.

The business leader who says he can't be at home because the business depends on him to be at work must ask if his values have shifted and if the shift is right. That man often says, "My wife can take care of the parenting. That's how this arrangement works." To a degree, the arrangement must work that way because both work and family require time and effort—not to mention the seasons of increased busyness that come with each. As a disclaimer, let me remind readers that I understand it might be the wife instead of the husband who is doing the providing—or both. My preference in describing it as the husband's role is simply based on the focus of this book—the absent father.

The question becomes one of balance. Often, dad mistakenly thinks he must do it all at work or that he can't afford to hire the help he needs the most, or that no one can do the job like he does. Following this line of thought is not the goal of this book. To pursue it further, I suggest reading *E-Myth Revisited* by Michael E. Gerber, among many other well-written books on focus while running a family business.

The change in perspective as to what matters to men as providers is a subtle slide into a quicksand that traps them into making justifications as to why they must be gone from the family.

If a dad is starting or running a family company or building his business, it can require a lot of time. While a season of extra hours is one thing, long hours tend to become the rule for most. Before long, the business becomes the priority rather than having the business for the purpose of providing for the family. In your role as father and businessman, are you primarily a provider for your family, or have you become a businessman whose end goal is to build the business and yourself? Of course, if asked, you would automatically reply, "This is all for my family." I hear this statement—this excuse—over and over.

For a father who is the primary provider, that proactive thinking process will help determine the work-life balance question. It changes the question from, "Should I spend more time at the office?" to "How can I build my business and still be an effective involved role model for my family and others?"

As business and career changes and opportunities come up, he might ask, "How will this decision affect my role as a father?" Those questions could be a basis for almost all business decisions that come along. Business people tend to not like to think this way because it upsets the status quo in the business setting. However, if they are really open to making both family and business work, it is amazing the creative opportunities that surface.

It also takes vulnerability because it requires going beneath the surface to evaluate motives, values, relationships, and what matters most in life. Finally, it may appear to be a risk, at first. If it changes schedules, priorities, and responsibilities, it requires letting go of control, power, and authority, all of which may only be in the mind anyway. In other words, it may require taking off the masks we develop as a result of our pride and ego. If he is willing to take that journey, often requiring wise counsel, the leader will find the rewards of a strong family and still have a strong business.

When a father is out of balance in his role within the family, it requires others in the family to compensate, and not always in healthy ways.

Chapter 11

Families Out of Balance

"Shame is a soul-eating emotion."

−C. G. JUNG, SWISS PSYCHIATRIST

"If how things LOOK is what matters, how things ARE will never be dealt with."

−ANONYMOUS

Based on my experience with clients, I can only assume that you, the reader, have been comparing notes with your own life, your parents, and the influences that have shaped who you are today. Understanding root issues such as these is the first step to bringing about change to the surface level of family and business life. I urge you to write out your own stories. It is by writing them that we give them the attention needed to fully grasp how they have worked in our lives.

Let's look at the different family dynamics that can arise when a father abdicates his leadership role in favor of being passive.

Problem Parenting Styles

Growing up, I often wondered why my dad—who most of the time was quiet, happy, and gentle—could suddenly be so angry and lose his temper, seemingly out of nowhere. Later, I learned he bore the brunt of mom's shaming as much as we kids did. Mom's expert use of shame and performance demands made an uncomfortable situation for dad. Who would want to be subjected to that?

His commitment to work allowed him an excuse to be gone. The more he was gone, the less he was involved in the day-to-day lives of us kids. He became an absent and unengaged father. I described this earlier as being passive. Unfortunately, this only gave more and more authority and dominance to my mom.

In fact, a passive father hates that his wife is dominant, yet he is precisely the one giving her the power, even if it is by default. Since dad had become passive in the home, mom began treating him in many ways like she treated us kids, controlling what he did, said, and how he looked. With her natural bent to safety, protection, and nesting, she stripped his masculine adventurous spirit.

Below are some leadership styles that create problems in both settings. They indicate a home setting but you can apply it to the work setting by inference. While I added thoughts to this list, it is based on work by Dr. Susan Forward.[1]

PROBLEM	RESULTS
MOTHERS	**SONS**
Mother as smothering /suffocating.	Expects he can get whatever he wants.
Mother as controlling	May see relationships with women as a power struggle to control or dominate him.
Mother as a victim. *(role reversal)*	Being placed in the role as a provider can create anger against women; a need to be mothered as an adult; or inadequate and helpless to meet his adult women's needs.
Mother as rejecter	Anger and frustrated at deprivation. Uses abuse to cover vulnerability.
Mother as abuser	Deep hatred and intense need of women.
FATHERS	**SONS**
Father as tyrant	Two responses: 1) Identifying with his father, the son learns to tyrannize and abuse people; May learn to always try to control women by hurting, scaring or demeaning them. 2) Becomes weak, helpless and a victim who is likely to continue to be dependent on mom.
Father as passive	May become too dependent on women, exhibiting a vulnerability and neediness.

If we recognize the problems of the past, it can help us find solutions for the present.

Performance-Based System

I grew up in Chicago in a loving, stable, blue collar family with strong Christian values. It was a good life and childhood, so don't hear me saying it wasn't. Nonetheless, these systems shaped me in ways that left an imprint that took years to deal with and overcome. They were generational in their impact imprinting relatives both before and after me. In my immediate family, it didn't affect us all the same. One of my sisters was shaped similarly to me. The other two had a different experience entirely. There were two dominant family systems in play—performance and shame—and it was obviously by knowing grandma that mom had learned them well from her.

Every Saturday morning, mom would get up very early to wash the clothes and hang them out in the backyard. She always complained about getting up so early every week. I vividly remember when I was about nine, asking her, "Mom, you don't have anything else going on today, why did you have to get up so early?" Her response: "If I don't get the clothes out on the line early, the neighbors will think I'm a lazy housewife." The shaping moment lesson I learned was: how things look matters more than how things really are.

Mom was very performance oriented, and this is a simple example. We are all performance-based; how we look, act, and sound matters to us and drives our whole society. But it matters to some more than others. It becomes their source of identity, acceptance, and value. What I additionally learned from mom is that what other people thought of her mattered a great deal so that, while she seemed controlling, it was actually others who controlled her life in many ways. A common phrase was, "What will the relatives (or neighbors) think?" I also learned years later that she wasn't trying to protect us kids from looking bad as much as she was protecting herself. Everything we did, said, or how we looked was a direct reflection on her. If we looked or acted bad, it was a shame to her own character.[2]

Shame-Based System

On top of her performance-based system, mom added her version of the shamed-based system she had learned. Not only did I need to perform to her standards, but *shame on me* if I didn't.

Regarding this system, one has to understand the difference between guilt and shame. I believe guilt is based on action taken as a result of choices. If I drive 20 mph over the speed limit and get a ticket as a result, I am guilty of making the choice to drive 20 mph over the speed limit. In this case, guilt is a fact, not a feeling. If I do not get caught, I may or may not feel the guilt as much, but of course, I am just as guilty of making the decision to break the law.

Shame, on the other hand, says my choices reflect my character. If I choose to speed, it says not only am I guilty, but my very character is defective—something is wrong with me. Shame belittles, destroys character and identity, and is, in essence, a tragedy of bullying proportions. C. G. Jung said, "Shame is a soul-eating emotion."[3]

Where it gets a bit confusing is that the word guilt, as opposed to being guilty, may be similar to shame in that it is based on the feelings primarily concerning who we are, our character. Marilyn Sorensen said it succinctly: "Unlike guilt, which is the feeling of *doing* something wrong, shame is the feeling of *being* something wrong."[4]

Recently, my wife and I rented a car in Amsterdam and drove to a small village near the sea. While being inquisitive as a tourist, I drove our compact rental car slowly through a passage so narrow between buildings that the rear wheel became stuck on a concrete step. It was that tight. While a wonderful angel of a man helped me maneuver out of it (to correct my bad choice), another elderly man stood by my window looking me in the eye, wagging his head with that look of "you stupid fool" and muttering, "tsk, tsk, tsk." The shame seemed to be oozing out of his pores and flowing over the whole car with me and my wife inside it.

If this had happened years earlier, I would have felt so flawed. To him, my bad choice seemed to reflect my obviously defective character, and therefore, my behavior was only to be expected. Since I now understood this for what it was, I saw him as comical and couldn't resist the retort in turn, "Shame on you for not helping." After all, if you're not part of the solution, you're part of the problem. By the way, I loudly praised and thanked the angel for his help and good spirit. I hoped the comparison had a positive impact on the head wagger, but I also know such behavior is typically deeply ingrained and not easily changed.

As Ray Bradbury said in *Fahrenheit 451,* "But you can't make people listen. They have to come 'round in their own time, wondering what happened and why the world blew up around them."

Shame is so widespread and common that we not only don't recognize it as detrimental, but we allow it to govern us unaware and to such a degree it has become a general characteristic of an entire culture. We shame others primarily because we believe that shame will change and ultimately stop a person's unwanted behavior. I want to believe that was my mom's motive in using shame: to make me feel bad enough to behave up to her standards next time. To a degree, shame does control behavior. However, what I know is that *shame may alter behavior, but it does not change the root of behavior.* Therefore, shame does not accomplish its intent.

Although my mom's shame was designed to make me feel bad, it was not accompanied by instruction to help me understand why it was wrong. As is true with so many young people, when I got away from home, I did whatever I wanted because I was now free—not from the rules, but from the shame. As a result, I did not always show a good sense of discernment or judgment because *my understanding of right and wrong came from unexplained shame,* not from reason or even from the wonderful value system that my family's lives were based on. Let me say that another way: I believe this kind of shame is antithetical to everything the Bible teaches! All those factors contributed to me being rather confused or uninitiated when it came to making wise decisions and why it may have taken me longer to develop a sense of confidence, self-worth, and identity.

As a result of shame, I learned to react using various defense mechanisms, but mostly I just felt confused and really bad. In chapters 13 and 14, we will discuss the interesting phenomenon known as transference. Much of that comes into play in a shame-based system. Like my home, my mother grew up in a home where measuring up to standards of behavior mattered to her parents, my grandparents. Some of that was simply about learning those standards and some was about being shamed in the learning process.

Without her knowing it, I believe mom was acting out of both learned standards and being shamed herself. As a result of her experience, she was transferring those standards to me as a defense mechanism of her own.

Cycle of Shame

I have developed the following Cycle of Shame to help understand the flow. You will see a great deal of similarity to the Cycle of Anger presented in chapter 15.

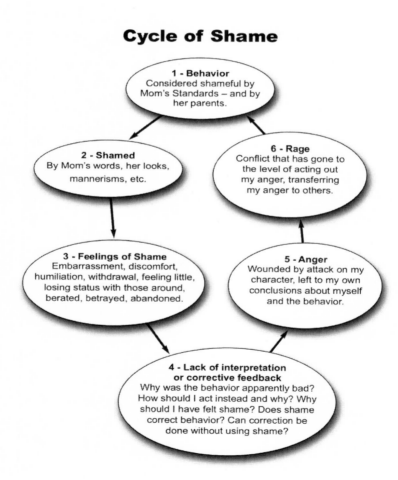

Cycle of Shame

1 - Behavior
Considered shameful by Mom's Standards – and by her parents.

2 - Shamed
By Mom's words, her looks, mannerisms, etc.

6 - Rage
Conflict that has gone to the level of acting out my anger, transferring my anger to others.

3 - Feelings of Shame
Embarrassment, discomfort, humiliation, withdrawal, feeling little, losing status with those around, berated, betrayed, abandoned.

5 - Anger
Wounded by attack on my character, left to my own conclusions about myself and the behavior.

4 - Lack of interpretation or corrective feedback
Why was the behavior apparently bad? How should I act instead and why? Why should I have felt shame? Does shame correct behavior? Can correction be done without using shame?

It took me years to deal with the negative impact of being shamed, let alone to understand the source of my defensive behavior that would only add fuel to the shame. I wondered why I was such an angry young man. Looking back now, I can better understand why so many young men are angry today. Shame is that pervasive.

Chapter 12

Business Out of Balance

"I sometimes ask myself: 'How do I save the best part of myself for my kids?' When I'm home, it's crucial that I'm totally present, and the no screen rule helps me do this."

−RYAN SMITH, CEO

As a business and life coach, a large number of my clients were from family-owned businesses. It was through this setting that much of my personal revelations about the universal influence of the father really became clear. Even though my clients had very different businesses and circumstances from one another, they would have similar and consistent patterns within their family dynamics.

When I ask dads what their relationship was like with their kids when they were young, they often say things like, "Oh, I was too busy working to have time for them," or as the kids got older, "They were around me all the time. I didn't teach them the business—I just expected them to get it."

Whether you have a family business or a job working for someone else, there are factors involved that apply to all parenting issues.

The Generational Breakdown

An all too common, well-documented scenario exists for family businesses: Briefly, one generation rolls up its shirtsleeves and gets to work building a business to success. But the next generation doesn't follow suit because they don't have the same motivation, haven't been trained or equipped, or are just not interested in running a business. This generation proceeds to run the business into the ground, all while living it up, spending whatever profits the business had accumulated. Then the third generation is left with nothing, just as the first generation had. In the best cases, they or their children then become interested in the potential, roll up the proverbial shirtsleeves, and get back to work rebuilding the business to success.

This pattern occurs often enough it's commonly referred to as, "Shirtsleeves to shirtsleeves in three generations."

When we look at the circumstances that cause this cycle, we can clearly see the second generation of kids being set up to do precisely what they do, the way they resist and take for granted following mom and dad into their business. The parents who spent so much time working in and on their business with their sleeves rolled up, had little to no time for motivating, training, loving, or getting to know their offspring. Perhaps the only compensation to their children was to give them whatever they wanted as a substitute for giving themselves. The drive to provide became the need to be successful. This leaves the second generation with a lack of motivation, a lack of training, and a lack of deferred gratification.

Business author John Ward goes into great detail concerning all aspects of the "shirtsleeves" phenomena, and I agree with and applaud his conclusions and that of others who have studied this field so well and clarified the issues involved in succession. Ward makes it crystal clear that "the most critical issues facing business-owning families are family-based issues more than they are business-based issues."[1]

As should be evident by now, I go one step further in saying the *absent, uninvolved father principle* is at the root of both family- and business-based issues.

There are many cases in which the father does not take the proper leadership over his children in the family business. In such cases, the sons and daughters typically make their own moral codes.

One such story stands out. It is the ancient Hebrew story of the prophet Eli and his two sons. Their role as priests was a virtual business set up where they were in charge and each son could inherit his role from his father. Eli's problem was that he knew what he needed to do as the father of unruly sons, but he couldn't bring himself to do it. See if you find any modern day comparisons in this summary by author Tony Stoltzfus:

> Eli had a problem: his sons were out of control. He had put them in influential positions under his leadership, but they flaunted the rules and became increasingly unethical. When people came to give their offerings to God, Eli's sons would dip into the pot for their own personal use. If objections were raised, they would threaten to take whatever they wanted by force. Eli's sons acted as if the things God's people had placed sacrificially on His altar were their own. God was not pleased.
>
> While his sons were the ones who had cast off all restraint, Eli was in charge, and God held him to account for failing to lead. He still had one last chance to change.
>
> But by that time, Eli had lost hope. He acknowledged that God was speaking, but in despair simply replied, "It is the Lord; let him do what seems good to him." Not long afterward, Eli's two sons were both killed, and the ark of God, the centerpiece of Eli's ministry,

was lost. Eli himself fell over and died of a broken neck when he heard the news. All these disasters came to pass in a single day.[2]

As you can see, this problem of ineffective fathers and kids deciding their own moral codes is not new. In this case, the outcome was quite extreme and conclusive. In what ways are you encouraging the same story in your family and/or business, and what do you want to do about it?

Systems vs. Relationships

Each of the families that hired me for business coaching had major issues that were tearing them apart. They all knew, or assumed, improvements could be made to their workflow management, accounting practices, HR policies, marketing, customer retention, mission and purpose, and everything else about business systems. After all, if they were having problems, there had to be areas they were not seeing, understanding, or managing well.

Their businesses were not fun places to be for employment or for doing business because of people problems—relational issues. Those issues, in turn, had ways of tearing apart the aforementioned systems.

With one client in particular, I was called by the son...

> We were making progress on dealing with the roadblock between him and his father who owned the business—the roadblock was why he called. As a small local business, they had landed contracts with huge international conglomerates and had been very successful. Times were good, and good times tend to make systems seem almost unnecessary. The attitude that resonates at this point in a company's life is, "We're doing great as things are, we're making money, growing our staff, facilities, and product, and we don't see anything that is not working well." Clients either deny they have problems or the problems keep getting

pushed aside because things are going well. Actually, this may be the very best time to identify areas needing attention and dealing with them.

But now times have changed, and the company needed to make some procedural changes to stay up with the changing demands of the clients. Staying current is a business systems concern. But his dad was more interested in protecting the business as it had been and saw his son's attempts to update the business as threats to his leadership and control. As a result, they were losing contracts fast.

The good times had become desperate. Any discussions turned into arguments causing defensiveness, blame, and accusations, lack of direction, lack of decision making, and more loss of business. Dad was saying to his son, "I don't trust you." The son had major responsibility over certain aspects of production, staff, accounts, and policies. Dad withdrew almost all of those assignments in an attempt to regain control but in the process lost even more control. He was desperate and his son was hopeless. Mom felt conflicted, agreeing with her son but committed to her husband. Ultimately, she chose her husband and reinforced the vote of no confidence in her son.

Neither the father nor the mother was willing to have a conversation with me or anyone else. They were not even civil to their son. He followed all the steps outlined later in my chapter on reconciliation with a humble heart, but they would not listen. The son concluded he had two options: continue to fight a losing battle and see the business fall apart around him, or bid his father goodbye and strike out on his own. Neither was an option he wanted. This particular son was brilliant when it came to their product services, business systems, HR concerns, and management. If only his father could have seen that. The son finally bit the bullet, said goodbye to his father and his company, and set up a similar company that was able to meet the changing times of his industry with great success.

In this case, separating the two became a wise solution. His dad's business could continue in its struggle without him since he had been forced out anyway. He could begin a new business using his expertise without conflict. Then he could focus on the connection with his father without the entanglement of work and the power struggle coming from it.

Until he could understand this perspective, the biggest struggle this client had was leaving his father to start another business. He knew he could do it, but it felt like a betrayal, running away, or abandoning his father. He became conflicted by tying the business to the kinship.

This matters more than the business matters. The business is about what we do. The relationships are about who we are. Whether to stay and fix the business or leave and start a separate business is not the question. In either case, the goal is to reconcile. Unfortunately, most tend to choose the business solution out of ignorance, anger, frustration, hopelessness, or giving in, and they never move towards reconciliation. That is the real tragedy.

Section 3

Father Uninvolvement in the
Past Affects the Present

Chapter 13

When the Past Invades the Present

"During transference, people turn into a 'biological time machine.'"
—MICHAEL CONNRE, PSY.D

Sam was in a job he loved. For him, graphics was second nature and this advertising firm was his dream come true. He loved the setting, the hours, and the pay, and he got along well with everyone. In an office down the hall there was one woman in particular whom he enjoyed. Jane was about twenty years older than he was, and they seemed to have a natural connection of understanding each other's wit and way of thinking. They hit it off almost from the day he was hired.

One day at mid-morning break time, he and several other employees had wandered into Jane's office to hobnob about the weekend's big NFL football game. It was a fun conversation and included some jib-jabbing comments poking fun at each other. Jane was in the swing of it when she said, "That quarterback fumble looked like Sam the other day when he was trying to fix that copier—ink all over the place."

Everyone laughed. Except Sam.

Normally he would have too, but this time something set him off. He got red in the face, threw his notebook across the room, and stormed out and down the hall.

Everyone was shocked, wondering what was going on with Sam. This was so unlike him—or was it?

We have all witnessed the extreme reaction of a person (maybe ourselves) to what we thought was a rather minor incident. Yelling, crying, accusing, blaming, even getting physical, their words often completely at odds with what actually happened. We are shocked and taken aback. Where on earth did that come from?

The Trap of Transference

Transference is our response of anger toward a person in the present who triggers an unrelated experience in our past that caused pain. But unlike a benign reminder of the past, transference is not a conscious memory. We don't recognize the true stimulus is in the past, so our mind reacts as though it's all happening in the present. Like Sam's, this reaction often comes out as overblown anger or unrealistic demands of unsuspecting and undeserving people who are not even aware of what is happening, like those in Jane's office party.

PhD Ben Dattner refers to transference as "seeing the present through the lens of the past."[1] Essentially, we are reenacting our family dynamics from childhood, where we treat our boss as a parent, our peers as siblings, our employees as children, and our performance reviews as report cards, to see fairness, equity, and resource allocation according to the way things were done in our families. However our childhoods taught us to respond to conflict, criticism, shame, correction, love, sharing, respect, will return to us in moments where circumstances in later life trigger that early life memory.

Those original events were traumatic and may have been patterns of mistreatment which developed into negative agreements (more on this in chapter 14) that we unknowingly form as beliefs about ourselves that are not true, and we make them against the people who perpetrated the events. For instance, my client, Don, had formed a negative agreement with himself because of his father's words that he could never do anything good enough. His father said it often enough that Don hated his father for saying it *and* came to believe it about himself as being true—to the point of not being able to handle success.

This is not something we will be aware of in the moment, so it's important to take time to reflect when moments of anger take place to recognize that it may be transference bubbling to the surface. If so, it can help us react appropriately to the present situation, break the negative agreements against ourselves and the perpetrator, and prepare for future instances that will inevitably occur again. Breaking negative agreements is essential to breaking the pattern of transference.

Not only will each of us react with transference at various times, but we will undoubtedly be the trigger to someone else's transference, and we should try to recognize that as well.

How does this topic fit a book on absent fathers? In chapter 7, we talked about the roles of fathers and mothers in giving identity, protecting, nurturing, encouraging, and providing for their children. Therefore, the roots of most transference occurs under their influence, or lack thereof.

Transference has such a powerful lifetime hold on us because the root memories involve times of being rejected, embarrassed, shamed, prejudiced, betrayed, abandoned, and otherwise not chosen. These are words of great pain, usually associated with suffering. They are words that primarily come through one's parents or others closely associated with them. The events may happen through obvious abuse or perhaps in ways so subtle no one would ever consider them as abusive. What matters is how the event was perceived by and impacted the child.

Just as it is the father's role to help a child find his identity, Sam needs guidance to help him acknowledge his behavior and address its roots so that he and the whole team can move forward in a healthy way. When a true leader—even those not in an official leadership role—sees conflicts that are more than what they ought to be, or meltdown emotional reactions that indicate hurting people, they have a duty to step in, to come alongside, to console, to help. Only by finding the source of the negative reactions can the hurting individual uncover the influences that are masking their true self and progress toward the clarity and healing they need. This is the ultimate job of we all have, to be responsibly caring for others. Not coddling or enabling or excusing, not intimidating or berating or avoiding—caring.

In some cases, what the hurting individual needs may be far more than the father, leader, or friend is capable of doing, but helping is not all or nothing. In the holy tradition of the Good Samaritan, we are called to do what we can, when we can, with what we have, for those whose paths we cross.

As we have established in the preceding chapters, there is a dire need for this role to be filled in our society. As fathers and as representations of fathers, men have a unique opportunity to serve a deep primal need that all individuals carry, whether any of us are consciously aware of it or not. This is the true calling, but one that is sabotaged by physical absence and passivity.

Rather than denying this, let's own it and begin to move forward.

Transference in the Family

"Stop treating me as if you're my mother!"

This is a common expression of transference that comes from marriage, including my own! My mother was the dominant person in my childhood home. As I described in more detail in chapter 11, she often used the technique of shame to try to discipline and shape me. Remember, even though she was trying to make me a better person, shame attacks one's character rather than changing or correcting one's behavior. The constant attacks on my character were painful for me. As I grew up, this treatment created a distance in my love for my mother. I always tried to treat her with respect and love, but it was difficult for me to really love her, or to want to hug her and be with her. When shame was used, it made me feel less of a person, and I wanted to be somewhere else.

Then I married my wonderful wife, Kay, and things were different. She does not shame anyone (though we all do to some extent, it's not as a typical response or identifying characteristic). However, there were times she innocently said or did something that reminded me of my mom's controlling or shaming ways. I may or may not have recognized it as transference at the time, but my reaction was essentially to stiff-arm her and push her away.

While I didn't understand it at the time, those experiences triggered memories of my past that caused me renewed pain and more shame. When they happened, I may have gone silent, gotten irritated, or even lashed out. Kay was always surprised, not knowing what she had done, and it was necessary for us to talk about it so we both knew and understood what was going on. This was more true and prevalent in the earlier years of our marriage before we both learned to spot the triggers and appropriate responses. I learned to recognize this for what it was (transference) and *usually* dissociate it from the past.

One thing I told Kay was that, if and when I got mad, it was not about her, and I was sorry that it sounded as if it was. I love her for who she is, and while she may have triggered those transferences at times, she was not the cause of my response—I was. That doesn't mean it was always easy for me to open up and talk about it, but when I did, it always helped to clear the air rather than letting it smolder.

Now here is a significant factor: for marriages in which one or both partners experience a level of transference (and they all do!) but they choose to ignore it rather than manage and resolve it, the relationship can deteriorate into dishonoring one another.

Dishonoring, degrading, disrespecting, humiliating, and other similar behaviors can become a root for a seething anger that, if not addressed, will spread until it destroys the relationship and roles of husband and wife, the parenting of their children, and even their views about men and women altogether.

Transference in the Workplace

"I get really uptight when my boss walks in. He scares me."

An employee who has this reaction is unlikely to connect their feelings to the notion that their boss reminds them of their strict demanding father, a man who was either working away from home or, when he was around, was a tough disciplinarian. The sight of him triggers the response to prepare to be in trouble.

Transference can occur the other way as well, from boss to employee.

Mike, the owner of a mid-size engineering firm, began to experience conflict with his secretary, Linda, with whom he had gotten along really well for several years. Mike described how Linda had begun to question his decisions in challenging ways with great detail. Since she had been there long enough to know the business well, many of her questions had value and were worth considering, but it was the constant barrage and seeming superior attitude that were unnerving him. Not having the appropriate interpersonal tools and being unable to respond appropriately, he felt his only solution was to let her go. To him, they were not a match.

After he did so, Mike contracted with me to evaluate this experience. After he described it in some detail, I asked my inevitable inquiry: "Mike, describe for me what it was like as a child in your home and the relationships you had with your father and other family members." So often, these experiences from the past feel shaming, embarrassing, or private, and a person will not go there without help. They have to see it is both safe and purposeful. The usual response is, "What does that have to do with my business problems?" But I had already shared some of my experiences in a vulnerable way, so he knew the sort of information I was interested in. It also gave him permission to be vulnerable in the same way.

Looking back through his experiences growing up, he described his father as a good provider who did things with his kids and was a gentle man who they all loved. However, in those memories, Mike could see his father was not the decision maker, the disciplinarian, or the leader that a father is expected to be. Whether intentional or not, he had given all those responsibilities to his more dominant wife and had become passive, or had always been passive from generations preceding.

Granted, those thoughts were not original for Mike, I had explained passivity to him to bring clarity and understanding of family dynamics. He said, "Yep, that describes our family exactly." The more he understood it, he admitted, "Just like my dad, I've been captured by passivity, both then and now."

Mike had an older sister who closely resembled his secretary's questioning and demanding ways. They both appeared to Mike as being jealous of him, what he had, and the responsibilities he had been given as an only son then and as the boss now. As kids, he remembers his sister nagged and berated him. Now, as adults, it hasn't changed. He is unable to respond to her demands or be around her.

As Mike reminisced about the agony of dealing with his sister, he realized he had dealt with his secretary in the same way. He had allowed the condition to build into conflict and was not able to resolve the issues. His experience with both women made him feel inferior, incompetent, and stressed—the same feelings as an adult and a boss that he had as a boy.

Mike realized through this evaluation that, as a father himself, he was emulating his own father's behavior in all those same ways. He had become as passive as his father. He was virtually giving permission to those around him to take over for him, even though he was in positions of responsibility. He was not addressing issues as they came up, but was stuffing them until he exploded. He was doing this to his wife, his sister, his oldest son, and his secretary.

We spent our time clarifying the transference scenario and the personalities involved, understanding how he was contributing to the conflict and allowing it to continue, and learning new tools of communication and leadership management. He moved from blaming and accusing these two women to understanding and accepting his own role and responsibilities. His behavior had been a generational problem—a stronghold that was sustained through transference and that he was passing to the next generation.

Any one of us may have this or some other equally impactful reaction to someone at work without understanding why. Sometimes the negative event from the past is recalled and sometimes not. That's what makes transference so tricky. Most of the time we can't see it happening, and even when we do, that doesn't magic away the strong negative reaction imposed on us by our subconscious.

Transference can happen across any relationship dynamic: employee to boss, boss to employee, employee to employee, employee to customer. Imagine all the possible miscommunication in the workplace based on the transference of memories from every person. It makes me wonder if anyone is ever reacting to present circumstances alone. And yet, our normal, typical response to conflict is to look at, draw conclusions from, and try to fix present circumstances. It's like putting bandages on cancer.

In most work settings, family is not actually present when transference raises its ugly head. In the case of the family business, the opposite is true. Due to the level of intimacy between individuals, transference can become even more dicey. This dynamic goes on to affect everyone connected to the business—employees or customers. Even though they aren't family, they will interact with a transference atmosphere that is dialed to ten, which is all the more reason to be aware of triggers. If we can recognize them right away, we can begin to deal in reality rather than pain from the past.

Dealing with the entanglements of transference is like negotiating a jungle. We'll see next that it comes with many root causes, implications, and manifestations.

Chapter 14

The Truth about Transference

"Now with God's help I shall become myself."

— KIERKEGAARD

Let's clarify the definition of transference to be our *response of anger* toward a person or event in the present that triggers an unrelated experience in our past that caused us pain.

Those past incidents can be ones that assaulted our character, personality traits, skills, physical appearance, rights, intelligence, and the list goes on. In most cases, they attacked our sense of self-worth, who we are, our identity, and our value as a person—things we must protect because someone didn't protect us in the past, especially as a child.

The source is usually a person or persons in authority, such as parents, older siblings, teachers, caregivers, and the like. The attacks were against such primal foundations of who we are that our subconscious won't let them go. It ties the incidents to the slightest connection in the present, causing us to respond in ways that confuse everyone around, including ourselves.

Dr. Samuel Peeples said it this way: "The circumstances of life, the events of life, and the people around me in life do not make me the way I am, but reveal the way I am." When we are young and impressionable, negative experiences contribute to forming our opinion of ourselves. Most identity anger comes from transference. As a result, we believe and accept things about ourselves that aren't true and apply them to our lives. We come to agree with them. These beliefs are called negative agreements or strongholds.

Dealing with the entanglements of transference is like negotiating a jungle. There are many root causes, implications, and manifestations. They all impact relationships, but in reality, they come from false messages we have been told, or from our own individual ego, pride, and self-protection mechanisms. We can better understand it by looking further into the four overlapping ways we see ourselves in light of our parental relationships.

Negative Agreements, Negative Vows, Strongholds, and Limiting Beliefs

"I am nothing like my dad!"

"I will never be anything like my dad."

The first statement is a *limiting belief.* The second is a *negative vow.* We've all heard them (or said them!), often in great anger or defiance. It is interesting that most of us who make such statements eventually become just like the person we vow not to become. Even others listening to us will say, "Maybe not, but from what I see, you are just like him." What makes it a limiting belief or a negative vow is that the son formed an opinion out of his experience that ended up driving his emotions, behavior, and attitudes, which in turn, shaped, controlled, and limited his life.

"I'm not pretty. My mom always told me that."

This person has decided her mother is right. She is not pretty. She has made a *negative agreement* with her mother. That agreement has affected her sense of self, how she dresses, her femininity, the people she chooses as friends, and her outlook on life.

"I'm not going out for track. When I told the coach I was interested, he smirked and said, 'Well, if you really want to.' I just know I'm not good at that stuff."

These statements started as a *negative agreement* and became a *stronghold,* which developed into a *limiting belief.* They were said more out of resignation than anger, but the effect is the same. We agree to something someone else said about us, accept what they said as true, and allow it to control our lives. They become self-fulfilling prophecy, as mentioned earlier concerning the names people call us.

Negative vows and agreements are reactions to hurt, and they define who we are compared to some perpetrator (most commonly our mother or father) who has hurt us. They turn into *strongholds* when we choose to believe them or allow them to control our lives based on the painful emotional memories that started them.

When we make such an agreement, we don't realize we are making it. It comes from a dark place embroiled in emotions of fear, anger, and hatred. In the case of the other examples above, it may be the emotions of self-hatred, depression, or the resignation to a poor self-concept, typically based on comments and viewpoints of others. Because of the pain of the experience, we make the agreement in an attempt to distance and separate ourselves from the person. The problem with such agreements is that the opposite happens: they actually attach us to the person spiritually and emotionally through unforgiveness. It becomes a trap or a prison, where we are the ones being penalized, not them. They may not even have any idea of our concern or dislike for them.

Because these experiences that become strongholds and limiting beliefs are simmering under the surface, they are easily provoked and turn into times of acting out at any time when something or someone triggers the memory. I believe this is at the root of most domestic violence that we witness. The person with the memory explodes against another family member, blaming them for the current explosion without realizing where it came from.

This brings us back to transference and shows more clearly how it begins from a root of anger.

There is a betrayal in these negative beliefs—betrayal by others because no one stepped in to help the son or daughter understand and interpret life's bad, even cruel and perhaps evil experiences. When we recognize and allow these strongholds to continue in our lives we, in essence, betray ourselves. We allow anger, contempt, resentment, and pride to protect us from the hurt and from being hurt again. This is what puts us in a prison.

To take it one step further, we, in turn, betray others by our words and actions that create pain in their lives and cause them to accept negative agreements, vows, and limiting beliefs that become strongholds to them. This becomes a vicious cycle of pain that is observed, learned, and passed on from generation to generation unless it is recognized and stopped by intentionally saying, "No more."

Breaking negative agreements against one's mother and father or others in authority is essential. It is central to stopping the patterns of anger and transference with its random angry flare-ups in current life. It may be a struggle to identify the cause of pain, but having done so, breaking the bonds of strongholds can be just as painful. It requires forgiving and releasing the other person which, in turn, will release us from our prison.

When we are the perpetrator and have caused this to happen to our own children or others, we have an obligation to ask if and how we betrayed them and to ask for forgiveness. Not only do we need it, but it allows them to be released from their own prison as well.

Author Richard Rohr sums this up well:

> ...Revelation is about transforming history and individuals so that we don't just keep handing the pain onto the next generation. That tit-for-tat, quid-pro-quo mentality has controlled most of human history.

Exporting our unresolved hurt is almost the underlying
story line of humans, so you can see why people still
need healthy spirituality and healthy relationships.

If we do not transform our pain, we will most assuredly
transmit it.[1]

Addressing Transference

We are used to seeing people throw tantrums or become defensive, huffy,
angry, or quiet. We wonder what got into them when the circumstances
didn't warrant their response. In fact, the circumstances may have happened
many times before and they did not respond this way. Our usual response
is to avoid them until they cool down and move on without addressing it.
If we do confront it, we may not know what we are confronting and end
up dealing with the surface blow up rather than the root causes. In that
way, businesses, organizations, and families spend many hours working to
resolve conflict that doesn't exist.

So, the *first step* is to recognize that transference is most likely the
root. Once we have observed the behavior and tried to understand its
source, dealing with it is the *next* step.

What makes dealing with transference or any other behavior reaction
difficult is the confrontation that is necessary.

The typical response to conflict for most people is avoidance.
Avoidance allows the behavior to be both controlling and to pop up unan-
nounced. If we don't know what was behind the behavior that allowed it
to surface in the first place, our avoidance gives power of control to the
employee or family member: "Treat me right or I'll explode again, and I
know you don't want that." Since we don't know what triggered the behavior, we walk around as if on eggshells, hoping it doesn't appear again. This
is quite common at home and in the workplace. Appropriate confrontation
is not familiar for most of us.

The following is a true story from the pages of the DadsFirst prison work. It is a cautionary tale far beyond what the average person experiences whether the perpetrator or the recipient. Even so, there are lessons for each one of us to learn and apply.

Ali's Story
(Used with permission)

My name is Ali. I am forty years old and serving 346 (months) for second-degree murder. I helped kill a man in a senseless, cruel, and cowardly act of violence. I did this because of a deep anger of another person in my life.

When I was twelve, a seventeen-year-old bully picked on, beat and spit on me for eight months. I began to plot to kill him. I asked him many times why he beat on me, and he said because I wasn't white and was a gook.

One day I took a kitchen knife to do him bodily harm. God had different plans, and the kid didn't come to school that day. I put the knife away and the next day the abuse continued. I scraped up money to buy a bottle of mace but again, he didn't show up. He continued to beat on me. I hated him with a passion.

One day, I pulled a pocket knife on him when he bullied me. I started swinging it and chased him. Out of the blue, a stranger showed up and convinced me to put it down. It wasn't worth it, he said, despite my explanations. The bully ran off.

When I was seventeen, I ran into him again at a state fair. I was with a group of guys and confronted him, not caring who might see. He said he didn't remember me, but I could tell he did. By this time, I was bigger than him.

He tried to walk by me, but I pulled him back and hit him a couple of times. The anger I had for him swelled up to overflowing. I pulled a gun and put it in his mouth. He began to beg for his life and peed in his pants.

I got high from his fear. I tried to pull the trigger, but something told me not to do it.

For the last twenty-eight years, I have asked myself where this anger and rage came from. It has hurt a lot of people. One day, sitting in prison, I was listening to lesson five of this course, the part that says, "Remember, transference is your response of anger toward a person in the present who triggers an unrelated experience in your past that caused you pain.

That's when I realized what I was doing all along.

This was a big step for Ali, who had lived for the day he could take his anger out on his bully. He says it was God who intervened, and later Ali repented and forgave the bully.

We all have anger as a result of pain from the past. In Ali's case, there are several lessons to notice:

1. If we don't deal with anger it will explode sooner or later.

2. Ali did not have any strong mentors to guide him when his anger showed up.

3. Experiences that lead to transference and anger crush our identity and purpose in life.

4. We all go further into our anger than we need or ought to go.

5. Ali grew up with negative agreements and judgments about himself. They were reinforced rather than broken.

6. Anger clouds our ability to see clearly and understand what is happening to us.

7. It's never too late to turn around, confess our wrongdoings, forgive, and be forgiven and reconciled.

What would Ali's outcome have been if he'd had a present father to fill the role he needed in item 2? How would he have been able to avoid some of the later items? Without a present father, Ali began down the path of anger, which we will look at next.

Chapter 15

The Path of Anger

"People and circumstances don't make us angry; we make ourselves angry."

—DR. PAUL O.

*"Anger is a manifestation of a deeper issue...and that, for me,
is based on insecurity, self-esteem and loneliness."*

—NAOMI CAMPBELL

*"Really, what profit is there for you to gain the whole
world and lose yourself in the process?"*

—JESUS

The fundamental principle of father influence is that presence begets presence and absence begets absence. This causes the generational impact we witness. Following the legacy of absence, the impact splinters into various other observable truths.

Children who experience father absence develop the father wound, which begets pain and a void of identity, self-worth, and confidence. Remember, we've said that most all the problems in society can be traced back to the root cause of father absence. That is the root. This void leads to often unhealthy methods of coping that bring along more pain. All of this pain lays the foundations for a lifetime of transference triggers. These triggers then have their own twisted offspring, the telltale sign of transference in action: anger.

Path of Anger

The dictionary[1] defines anger as: *a strong feeling of annoyance, displeasure, or hostility.*

The synonyms do an even better job of defining the strong feeling: *rage, vexation, exasperation, displeasure, crossness, irritation, irritability, indignation, pique, annoyance, fury, wrath, ire, outrage, irascibility, ill temper/ humor, slow-burn, aggravation.*

Add to that from the Father Hunger course that we teach at DadsFirst: *mad, frustrated, ticked-off, fear, anxiety, hurt, pain, shame, embarrassment, feeling defective, or any combination of these feelings.*

Transference is one cause of anger, and *anger* covers a lot.

Here is the definition again: "Transference is your response of anger toward a person in the present who triggers an unrelated experience in your past that caused you pain."

When it comes to transference, anger is likely to occur in both the person experiencing the transference and the person who is the recipient of it. The experiencer is triggered and lashes out. The target, usually innocent and often unduly lashed at, first recoils in defensiveness but then will often counter with their own anger at the injustice.

And 'round and 'round we go.

As much as we wish, we cannot go back in time to change the fact that an individual experienced the father absence that created their wound. The absence might have happened in the past, but the wound has remained, traveling forward in time in the heart and mind of the individual. The wound, created in the past, exists in the present.

Heal the wound and anger dissipates.

But how do you heal wounds as deep as those caused by generation upon generation of absence and passivity—deep, enduring wounds of abuse and neglect?

To discover this, we must first fully understand the depths of struggle currently faced by the wounded and unravel the anger that holds them hostage.

Causes of Anger

We are all familiar with the phrase "like father, like son." This maxim has been ingrained in all of us. Knowing the son is like knowing the father. It's true for fathers and daughters as well, but it is more observable in sons.

All of our previous generations laid the groundwork that defines the different roles and expectations that we hold for men today, specifically around expressing emotions. Many feel pressure to internalize and repress their anger rather than express it.

In my observation, it appears less socially acceptable for men to show other emotions, like sadness or fear or crying. Think of the cringe-worthy and cliche parenting phrase, often used against boys, "Stop crying or I'll give you something to cry about." Not only is this intended to strike fear into the child who is expressing emotion, but it implies that physical pain is the only valid reason for crying, or that it is not "masculine" to cry.

So instead, the majority of men channel all of their emotions through their anger as a false sense of power, or as desperation and frustration over the fact they are not able to manage the situation.

Anger is a significant issue with men in general, but it is important here because of its devastating role in, by, and through the father. Homes, families, communities, workplaces, military, governments: all of these are affected by our fathers, either positively or negatively.

Effect of Anger

Henryk Wieja, M.D., points to studies[2] that show the level of risk for children to demonstrate pathological behavior of anger to another object increases based on the extent of father involvement.

- With an engaged father and a healthy marriage relationship and environment, the risk is low, at 5 percent.
- With an absent father and a single mother, the risk rises to 30 percent.
- When there is a bad parental relationship with an unengaged but present father, the risk goes up to 60 percent. In addition to the higher risk, it seems evident that the kind of behavior resulting from the child's anger would also be more severe.

Here is a visual version of the statistics:

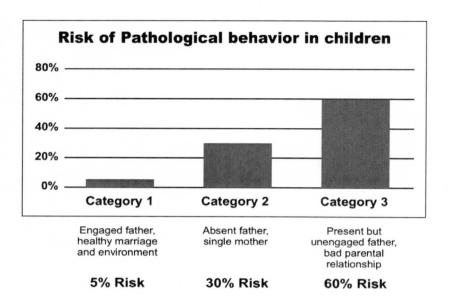

It is understandable how absence and passivity leads to the statistics cited in chapter 5. The unengaged father stokes his child's anger, which is more likely to be demonstrated by acting out.

Dr. Wieja also cited a study showing that there are five physical maladies in children of absent or uninvolved fathers: mental disease, heart failure, alcoholism/drug addiction, depression, and suicide.[3] with the only common factor for these maladies being an absent father. These maladies were stated regardless of other factors like socio-economic standing, access to health care, geographic location, and other considerations.

These are maladies that tend to result from extreme tension and stressful situations and relationships. Remember, being overly absent from home due to work, travel, hobbies, addictions, etc. is the same as being uninvolved and can, therefore, contribute to these responses in children.

In discussing these matters with others, I consistently get the pushback that they had a single mom and she did a fantastic job. It sounds as if I'm saying that's not possible. Remember, the statistics say 30 percent of kids with single moms exhibit pathological behavior. That means 70 percent do not, which is the group they fit into, thankfully.

The effectual impact of the statistics is to show the difference in risk of pathological behavior between the levels of father involvement or lack thereof, not the success rate of the mother, single or not.

The Cycle of Anger

It is very difficult to let go of one's anger. When we cannot forgive and let go, we become attached to the person we are angry with, both spiritually and emotionally. Often the action we need to take (forgiveness) feels like an injustice—we want that person to pay for what they've done. If we let go, we think they'll be off the hook, so instead we cling to our anger and stay bound ourselves.

Anger tends to be acted out in a progressive and cyclical manner. There are many versions of what is called the Cycle of Anger. This first one is representative of anger *in terms of behavior.*[4] Anger can begin anywhere in the cycle, but *betrayal* is often the trigger. They feel as if they have been betrayed and respond in kind. Their own wound may present as a feeling of being skipped over or demeaned, or a sense of a breach of trust, disloyalty, or being double-crossed. The slight of betrayal may be real or perceived.

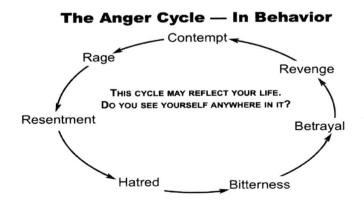

The Anger Cycle — In Behavior

Contempt · Rage · Revenge · Resentment · Betrayal · Hatred · Bitterness

THIS CYCLE MAY REFLECT YOUR LIFE.
DO YOU SEE YOURSELF ANYWHERE IN IT?

Once ignited, this feeling of betrayal must be addressed. If not addressed, it will be left to smolder and develop into a heart of *revenge*. Revenge wants to get back at a person (parent, sibling, supervisor, or peer), policy, business, etc. to get even for the wrong.

Revenge, when suppressed, turns to *contempt*. Contempt is also known as disrespect or scorn, which may be demonstrated by the father to family members or employees when he would rather be elsewhere. Or by the children or employees who have been treated in such a demeaning way as to respond with contempt or disdain. Contempt has a darker side to it, having the ability to set off an even deeper level of anger when uncontrolled or unattended. It grabs us and pulls us down.

One family business client of mine could have written this section. The grandfather, Peter, started the business and built it to a great reputation in its industry, with several hundred employees who were proud to work there. However, when he retired, his son, John, had a very lackadaisical attitude in becoming the CEO.

John was not a businessman and enjoyed the perks without really taking responsibility. As a result, things started to slip, mostly in attitude and reputation. The product was still good, but employees were losing trust and faith in the leadership. John's son, David, the founder's grandson, was now in his twenties with good ideas, schooling, and interest in entering the business. David wanted more authority to dive in and revive the company potential. It was a classic shirtsleeves to shirtsleeves phenomena. Despite his inability to lead, John, the new CEO, seemed threatened by his own son and stiff-armed his involvement. Soon, this frustrated and disappointed youngest son was caught in the Cycle of Anger.

David entered the cycle at *contempt* because of scorn for his father's unreasonable lack of trust and inability to lead. He began to demonstrate behaviors of *rage, resentment, hatred,* and *bitterness* around the Cycle of Anger rather than attempt to find workable solutions in the face of his inept father.

Each one of the words in the cycle is loaded with deep seated emotion, which can fester and grow. The words are interchangeable in meaning and order. Not only is a person in various stages of anger not nice to be around, but the negative attitude can affect and pull in those around him at home and on the job. Just as with the topic of transference, these behaviors need to be identified and addressed by the parents and leadership—and early, before they get out of control. I worked with John, the CEO, to help him understand absent father syndrome—from his father to him and he to his own son—but he saw it as a game with no real application and soon gave up trying completely. His dysfunction was too deeply ingrained.

While the steps in the Cycle of Anger occur in the heart and mind, it takes only a short step to turn them into action. The negative emotions and feelings are like gasoline to an engine, and feelings drive our actions. Feelings give us the ability to function in the world and to make things happen, whether for good or bad.

Granted, the Cycle of Anger, like Ali's Story, sounds rather extreme—and they often are, considering the DadsFirst Father Hunger course attendees are ex-cons, recovering addicts, or even prisoners in maximum security. They come from more extreme pathological behaviors,so this particular collection of terms is more likely to apply. In fact, when the words are introduced, the class members understand them immediately. Often, they can teach their own class on the impact and fallout of anger.

However, as in this case with John and David, it is not unusual for families and employees to also become bitter and act out by betraying and taking revenge on those in authority in some form or another. In truth, every person is vulnerable to these root words describing anger. Each of the cycle points can range from subtle to extreme, from imperceptible to acting out, from subtle passive/aggressive behavior to overt aggression.

Who knew that such a wide range of anger (road rage, rape, bullying, transference, lying, cheating, pride—you get the idea) could have its roots in father absence? It prompts me to repeat once more the statement from so many leaders: *nearly all the problems in our world today can be traced back to the root cause of fathers not being involved with their children.*

Problems in the family are systemic. Kids do not become rebellious and angry without a reason. A sense of betrayal on the job does not develop overnight. The father and business owner may not only be caught in the Cycle of Anger himself but is likely to also be guilty of allowing relationships, systems, and attitudes to go sour, giving a foothold to anger in the lives of those in his care. He has an awesome responsibility.

Another cycle focuses on the *emotions* rather than describing possible behavior.[5] It includes anger, which moves to self-destruction, to recovery, to hope, followed by disappointment, then reverting back to anger.

Emotions of Insanity Cycle

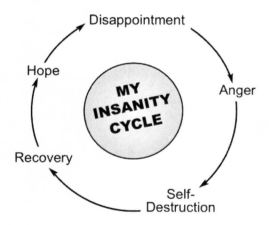

A final one to demonstrate here is called The Anger Cycle.[6] It describes *possible actual thoughts and actions* at each stage. Perhaps you can see yourself in each stage whether driving your car, working with staff, or doing chores around the house.

The Anger Cycle

Situation:
A driver cuts you off
in traffic

Thought:
"You idiot!"

Behavior:
Shout, aggression –
physical or verbal

**Process of
Thoughts
and Actions**

Symptoms:
Accelerated heart rate,
muscular tension, tremor,
rapid breathing

Emotions:
Rage, fury, anger

Seeing Our Own Cycles

It is not uncommon to hear people lament about the bad hand life has dealt them. These people are angry. They blame and accuse everyone about everything and accept no responsibility for their circumstances. All of us do this to some extent. We feel overlooked for a promotion, responsibility, or recognition that should have been ours. We imagine life is not treating us fairly. We get mad and look for something or someone to blame. Dads, you will see this in your kids, your relatives, and your employees—or you might feel it yourself. It is your job to first recognize it, second confront it, and third teach and resolve it, just like we discussed under transference in chapters 13 and 14.

We might hear, "You make me so mad." The truth is, no one can make us mad. We make ourselves mad. The earlier quote by Dr. Peeples indicates the trigger may even whisper words of accusation, suggesting maybe that's who we really are after all. This gives new light to the cycles of anger. Those difficult words are mostly within our sphere of control. We cannot control the words, actions, thoughts, and mistakes of others, but we can control our own.

In this regard, Richard Rohr said, "If we do not transform our pain, we will most assuredly transmit it."[7] This is important if we are concerned about personality and character traits that we don't like or that have affected our lives in negative ways—ways that we have the power to change. Rohr goes on to say if we don't learn this lesson "we will become inflexible, blaming, and petty as we grow older and we will pass on our deadness to our family, children, and friends."[8]

Anger is within the realm of our control, but we must learn how to do so.

I was as guilty of anger as anyone when behind the wheel of my car. When I was in my teens and twenties, it did not take much to set me off. I was an angry young man and my emotions would quickly work their way through each of the words in the Cycle of Anger, especially contempt leading to rage and revenge for seemingly mindless drivers. It seemed I could not let go of it, which only fostered it more.

Then something happened that helped to give me a different perspective. A good friend needed to drive to a certain location and wanted me to follow him. While en route, I observed my friend making some moves in traffic that would have enraged me under usual circumstances. However, this was my good friend, and surprisingly to me, my response was to say, "Whoa, buddy. What's going on? There must be a good explanation for that move."

I was concerned and understanding, and I both accepted and forgave him on the spot. Instead of going into conflict, I had a heart of love and even protection for him from other drivers. I tried to put myself in his place.

Instantly, I had an epiphany. I wondered how many times I had made similar moves that would have upset other drivers, only I "had reason" for making such a move. I could rationalize anything I did, whether right or wrong. Even dumb maneuvers of mine were justified for reasons of which those honking drivers had no inkling. Even worse, their honking would poke at my need to be right, making me want to get back at them—and so the cycle would go.

This was all a revelation for me, because my spirit felt so fresh and alive rather than the darkness of the elements of anger. I thought, "What if I were to think of all other drivers as if they were my best friend or a beloved family member?" I would have to begin seeing them in a new light, as if out of the box of all the negative characteristics and quirks I had used to label them.

I started doing this regularly and have now for many years. It allowed me to let go of the anger and actually enjoy driving again. When a driver cuts me off, I picture one of my kids as that driver and say "Whoa, sweetheart. That wasn't too swift, but you must have had a good reason. We're all okay, so keep going. We'll talk about this later." In an incident someone else obviously caused, I am more likely to help things go right by not blaming and accusing. The Cycle of Anger is becoming more distant—and not only behind the wheel.

The Greater Cycle at Play

Father absence results in the father wound, which results in pain, transference, and anger. Along with anger, the child may experience shame, insecurity, mistrust, anxiety, and fear. The specific emotions with which the child manifests their father absence wound will lead to their coping mechanism to fill the void.

The pattern created by the wound, resulting anger, and resulting coping mechanism is the primary factor that perpetuates the father absence cycle from generation to generation. This pattern is in large part what must be addressed in order to break the cycle and shift to active and intentional father presence.

We cannot diminish the impact our dads have on us, from chromosomes to emotional and personality characteristics. While it can be intentionally changed, a father's heart is shaped by that of his father, and his father before him. This reinforces how much a father needs to be aware of his impact on those around him and not just on his own comfort, behavior, and decision making.

Like absence, the effects of anger spread across all levels of society. To even begin to heal it, we must first see it for what it is, its complexities and interconnectedness. We will begin with the individual, specifically those where father absence has transferred extreme anger issues that play out in the most primal and visceral ways: individuals in prison.

Section 4

The Effect of the Uninvolved Father on Society

Chapter 16

Hope in the Halfway House

"The mass of men lead lives of quiet desperation."

—HENRY THOREAU

Many of the powerful moments I've experienced have occurred working with men and women in correctional facilities—everything from maximum security prisons to halfway houses. Such settings are like laboratories for observing anger in action and discovering its sources. This chapter is one such personal experience of anger in action.

It was a Tuesday evening in late April, and Chuck and I were on our way to a halfway house in a tough part of south Minneapolis. It was my first visit of this kind, and I was a bit (okay, make that a lot) nervous. Chuck was an old pro even then, having met with ex-cons for years already. His experience helped take some of the edge off, and I knew the material well that he would be presenting. Besides, my purpose was to simply observe and look for ways to improve the lessons. What did I have to be nervous about?

The neighborhood was filled with mansion-sized houses, once affluent but now repurposed into multi-family residences or homes for businesses and nonprofits. Others fell to the bulldozer to make way for modern homes, making the neighborhood quite eclectic.

While some of the original mansions had been restored to their original glory, our destination was worn out: faded and peeling paint, a sagging porch, and a front door littered with scuff marks. But even so, this former beauty had a new lease on life, this time as a halfway house.

We took the steps two at a time (probably not the best choice considering the state of the porch) and rang the seemingly silent doorbell. Still, the door opened and a tall, broad man appeared, large enough to fill the door frame.

Chuck knew him well and greeted him by name. "Hi, John."

The man sized me up and answered with a familiar but cautious, "Come on in, guys."

The gathering place was a dining room table that fit eight, but we squeezed fourteen chairs around it.

The men drifted in, casting me furtive glances, unsure of why a new guy was there. Some were transitioning from prison, others from drug treatment centers, but all were on their way to life on the outside. In almost all cases, the judge gave them an option: go through our ten-week program or spend more time in jail, a ruling that is both good and bad.

On the good side, it gives credence to the value and quality of our material. Even as a faith-based system, it is recognized by the court system. On the not-so-good side, our "captive" audience included some who were just biding their time and would likely find themselves back behind bars before long. We didn't even want to know what their crimes were.

A tough audience, to be sure.

The main theme of our ten-lesson program is, of course, fatherlessness. The judicial system has come to recognize the men who offend are under the influence of generations of crime, abuse, addictions, hatred, poverty, and ignorance, as well as a lack of direction, values, and identity. They understand that the root cause of fatherlessness must be addressed, and not by simply locking them up. There are many programs that deal with anger management, but unless one is confronted with the sources of anger, managing it becomes another case of putting bandages on cancer.

Of the twelve men sitting around the table that day—eight who were African Americans, two Latino, one Native American, and one white, all ranging in age from early twenties to forty-five years old—all of them were fatherless, most since birth. Given that Chuck and I are "in charge" in this setting, I was taken with the respect these men gave us compared to how they would have treated us prior to this setting. I believe they recognized the value of age, experience, vulnerability, and the mutual respect we showed them.

They either never knew their father or he left the picture at some point: abandoned them, got kicked out, was sitting in prison, or was dead. They had no relationship with their old man and didn't want one. Many were, at least biologically, fathers themselves, often with a few different women, and had little or no contact with their children.

And so goes the generational plague, the legacy of absence.

After some introductions and comments about last week's lesson, Chuck introduced the night's topic. It was the third lesson in the series called *My Father*.

"Today, we're going to talk about your relationship with your father, his impact on your life, and how to deal with any negative impacts of that relationship."

DaShawn, one of the younger men, erupted to his feet. "I'm not talkin' bout that (expletive) man. I hate him!" With eyes bulging and veins popping, he pounded the table, yelling while his violent past oozed out of every pore. He stomped off through the kitchen, while I was thinking he really just wanted to shoot us.

The house supervisor in the group made a start after him but let him go once it was clear his destination was the basement.

A few others didn't seem too surprised, "Don't mind him. Keep going."

Another started to get up, yelling, "No. DaShawn's right. This is BS! I ain't doin' it."

Tempers revved up instantly, and we had a powder keg ready to blow.

"That's enough! Sit down and shut up!" Obviously this behavior is a part of daily life, as the supervisor's voice cut through and cooled things down immediately.

Taking a deep breath of relief, Chuck proceeded to the next step, and in a few minutes pounding noises came up from the basement.

"He's banging out his frustrations on the punching bag down there," someone explained to our questioning looks.

Better the bag than me, I thought. It went on for several minutes while we talked, and before long, DaShawn walked back in as if nothing happened. Even though he stated earlier that he hated his father, he knew if he skipped out he would have to repeat the whole ten classes. He sat down and looked as if he really wanted to hear what was next. In fact, I got the impression that DaShawn realized his outbursts reflected his immaturity more than his masculinity. Eventually, that behavior gets embarrassing.

The lesson asked the men to identify positive and negative ways in which they were similar to their father and ways in which they were different. As if a switch was turned on, the men were drawn into this exercise with a lot of discussion and emotion.

"I never knew my dad," one of the older men said. His face displayed anger, disappointment, and perhaps feeling sorry for himself that he can't know how much he is alike or different from his father.

"What do you think about that, Tim?" Chuck passed the fellow's statement to me.

I leaned forward and addressed the man. "Have you ever heard other people in your family describe him, what he looked like, how he walked or talked?"

A faint nod came as he leafed through the pages in his memory.

"What did they say?"

He got the idea and started writing.

"And another thing," I added. "What would you *want* your father to be like? Some of those ideas will be okay to add, too."

He wrote some more.

For the next question, Chuck asked, "How did your relationship with your dad impact your fathering, relationships with women, co-workers, friends, and so on?"

More discussion followed—some very animated as the light bulbs came on with *aha* thoughts.

"Think about what you have discovered. Even with all the bad vibes, there are some positives that you could thank him for, positives you may want to continue with your kids or other people. There's always some good to find."

Chuck had their attention.

"Now let's think about some negatives you see in him that you may see in yourself, things you hate and want to stop." This was a new idea—that they could change their ways. "You might even want to consider pardoning him."

"No way, man," several said. "He doesn't deserve a pardon," and, "I'm not letting him off the hook."

Chuck was ready for this one.

"When you pardon your father for offenses of the past, it has a way of ending the pain. You no longer have to feel the memories or engage thoughts of hurts. You no longer have to provide a prison cell in your heart and mind for your hurtful father. It does you no good to keep him there. You can pardon. Choose to forgive.

"It takes a huge weight of anger and pain off your shoulders and gives you freedom to move on, just like getting out of a real prison or freedom from an addiction. Forgiveness is really for your benefit, not just your father's."

Concepts like this take time to sink in.

The next step was to invite them to write a "Dear Dad" letter.[1]

Whoa! The anger and hate rumbled right to the surface again. The benefits of pardoning hadn't sunk in yet. Talking about their dad is one thing, but writing a letter to him—forget it!

"You don't have to send it if you don't want to," Chuck assured them. "The healing is in the writing. Sending it or reading it to them is another. It's up to you."

"My father is dead," one said, appearing relieved that he wouldn't have to send it, or even write it, for that matter.

"Writing it is the important part," Chuck responds. "And you can always take it to the cemetery and read it at his grave site. It can have a powerful effect on you. I would like each of you to write this letter using the instructions on the back of your blank letter form and turn it in next week at our meeting."

More of them said, "No way," and, "I'm not doin' it."

From experience, Chuck knew that almost all would write it over the next few weeks. The men have tough-as-nails exteriors, but on the inside they are like puppy dogs. Some of the toughest melt the most.

We closed by having them write down some action steps to work on, and we primed the pump by suggesting phrases such as these to help them get going:

"I will call my dad, even tell him I love him—wow! Did I just say that?"

"I have lost touch with my dad, but I will write the letter anyway."

"I always said I am nothing like my dad, but now I see it. I'm just like him. I have some changes to make."

Surprising everyone at the table, DaShawn piped up: "I can own that one."

Lives Transformed

On the drive home, Chuck and I talked and compared notes. I confessed that the experience of being around such a volatile group was exhausting and a bit scary. You never know when someone is going to erupt. Like walking into a lion's den or ripping open fresh wounds. But seeing an exercise as simple as writing a letter transform a group of such hardcore men was amazing to witness. The reward was worth all the risk.

Individuals who have been wounded by father absence are not just found in prison—we're everywhere. And sadly, our father wounds don't just stay with us. As we saw with transference, they spread. To our loved ones, workplaces, and the strangers of society. To people around us we don't even know.

Chapter 17

When Anger
Spreads to Society

"Our lives begin to end the day we become silent about things that matter."
— MARTIN LUTHER KING, JR.

*"Our lives improve only when we take chances—and the first
and most difficult risk is to be honest with ourselves."*

— WALTER ANDERSON

Think back to chapter 11, where a father's absence or passivity creates a vacuum that requires the mother to modify her role in order to fill it. This results in further imbalance, one that affects the children's view of both their father and mother, as well as the way the father and mother view each other.

As this imbalance occurs within families and is perpetuated across generations, the impact against individuals is increased, as is the level of anger.

When a father is absent from the family, either physically or emotionally, the anger that manifests won't necessarily be directed at the father. The anger I witnessed in the halfway house applies to more than just fathers.

Just like the *My Father* lesson, DadsFirst also has a *My Mother* lesson and even a *My Child's Mother* lesson. The very practical application of these lessons really hits home because, so often, these relationships have contributed to their life of crime and/or addictions. Repeatedly, the men respond with, "No wonder I have so much trouble with the women in my life."

The trouble referred to here is hatred, which represents an extremely destructive case of transference. This kind of transference occurs outside of the typical scenario—from an individual to another individual in a specific isolated interaction. The magnitude of the transference grows to the point the individual transfers their past experience to an entire group. Instead of being a sporadic experience that occurs in the most heightened specific circumstances, the traumatic transference experience becomes constant—an ever present influence on the affected individual's beliefs and behaviors.

Misogyny and Misandry

The anger and transference experienced by individuals, whether children or spouse, due to absent or passive fathers and unbalanced roles, can develop into something far more sinister.

Transference may occur toward an entire group, and the anger may develop into hatred. Men may develop *misogyny*, hatred and exploitation of women, and women may develop *misandry,* the hatred and exploitation of men.

Misogynistic men and misandrist women choose to self-protect and exploit the opposite sex to satisfy their own physical needs and desires, considering the other as objects rather than individuals. Both result from anger toward the opposite sex.

The following chart illustrates how the actions of each fuel the flames of hatred toward the other.[1]

MISOGYNY Anger towards women	MISANDRY Anger towards men
• Degrading language directed to or about women. • Any gaze or speech that treats women as objects, not persons. • Jokes told in and out of their presence. • Indulging in fantasies. • Pornographic obsessions. • Unwanted advances, escalation to harassment/rape.	• Engaging in "male-bashing". • Belittling a man's character and performance. • Jokes told in and out of their presence. • Using men for sex or other types of objectification. • Cutting men down in anger. • Escalation to contempt or disdain.

My focus is to look at this source of anger to understand some of its roots.

First of all, misogyny and misandry are *strongholds* that grip and affect a person's thoughts and behaviors. In addition, such strongholds often do not start with the individual, but have likely been passed down through generations of ancestors. They are typically reinforced by one's mother and/or father where the real bias is rooted and reinforced. This parent/child relationship is so powerful that the biases are received as betrayals and are expressed through anger. When observing people with a stronghold such as misogyny, it may not look like anger—in fact, they may justify it by saying they are "having fun." However, its roots are in anger.

Individuals with these sources of anger can be observed by the choice of their words, the focus of their conversations, and their behavior, as noted in the chart above.

Secondly, this behavior is destructive to individuals, families, and the workplace. Once observed, regardless of its source, it *must* be dealt with. Anyone who witnesses this behavior must object and speak up. In the #MeToo/#TimesUp movement that caught fire in October 2017, many women who were mistreated through misogyny gained strength from each other and spoke up. As a result, many prominent men were fired from their jobs when accused of sexual harassment.

While intervention like that may stop the surface behavior, it is only the individual man or woman gripped by the stronghold that must stop it at its roots since that is where it resides. That will not happen without first of all *awareness and understanding* of the core problem. This often requires confrontation and perhaps professional intervention. Betrayals cannot usually be changed without understanding how the person was betrayed, usually in childhood, followed by *breaking of those negative agreements, accepting and then releasing the shame* surrounding the resulting behaviors with a contrite heart, and then *forgiving and being forgiven* for words and behaviors that have wounded people on both sides of the betrayal.

For centuries, those in power who've observed the behavior have chosen to ignore it. The damaging effect on individuals and our society—and that we will continue to have unless we choose to take action to end it—cannot be understated.

If the misogynist is the father, business leader, or other fatherly mentor or figure, hopefully he, too, will be confronted by an authority with enough power to get him to listen and take action to stop and change the behavior in his own heart, in those within his sphere of influence, and to bring healing to those who have been negatively impacted.

Here is the official word from the US Equal Employment Opportunity Commission:

> It is unlawful to harass a person (an applicant or employee) because of that person's sex. Harassment can include 'sexual harassment' or unwelcome sexual advances, requests for sexual favors, and other verbal or physical harassment of a sexual nature.
>
> Harassment does not have to be of a sexual nature, however, and can include offensive remarks about a person's sex. For example, it is illegal to harass a

woman by making offensive comments about women in general.

Both victim and the harasser can be either a woman or a man, and the victim and harasser can be the same sex.

Although the law doesn't prohibit simple teasing, offhand comments, or isolated incidents that are not very serious, harassment is illegal when it is so frequent or severe that it creates a hostile or offensive work environment or when it results in an adverse employment decision (such as the victim being fired or demoted).

The harasser can be the victim's supervisor, a supervisor in another area, a co-worker, or someone who is not an employee of the employer, such as a client or customer.[2]

This legislation is a wonderful thing that has protected countless individuals who would have otherwise been left without recourse, but it is not a solution to the fundamental problem of hatred that goes back generations.

A Culture of Anger

Our society functions as a result of individuals communicating, coordinating, cooperating, and collaborating—the same individuals who have experienced wounds, and may have developed misogynist and misandrist views and behaviors because of them. These wounds, views, and behavior affect the individual's sphere of influence until we have a culture poisoned with anger and hatred.

When anger and hatred of men and women becomes commonplace, it become masked by normalcy. Misogyny and misandry then become all the more sinister—like passivity—because it is right in front of us but dismissed by the majority as "the way things are." It is so pervasive that all of society is decaying as a result.

If you've ever seen advertising from the early twentieth century, you'd recognize blatant and unapologetic demeaning depictions of women. In the late twentieth century and early twenty-first century, the pendulum began to swing the other way and depicted men, often specifically fathers, as the most incompetent, bumbling, and ineffective people on the planet. These commercials, shows, and films were likely leveraging the millennia of unequal treatment of women by men, but does not do well in combating the strongholds of misogyny and misandry.

If we ever want to heal—ourselves, our families, our society—we must stop the generational cycles that hold us hostage and address the root problem lying right in front of us.

Chapter 18

Addressing Our Roots

*"Children grow up loving their parents; as they grow
older they judge; sometimes they forgive them"*

—OSCAR WILDE

By now, the connection between all of these elements should be clearer. Father uninvolvement, whether played out through absence or passivity, distorts the developing identity of the individual and creates a wound that produces hurt and anger. Over the course of the wounded individual's life, the anger they feel is transferred to others and becomes a cycle. As the anger spreads, it creates larger issues society-wide. As this cycle of anger spreads, it furthers the cycle of fatherlessness for generations.

This damaging cycle is often compounded by major historical changes within a specific nation and culture, creating larger-scale issues that make recognizing the fatherlessness crisis even more difficult. When it's happening to everyone, it's harder to see the problem. It becomes normal—just the way life is. We often don't question it or have the hope left to believe that there's a more fulfilling way to live.

It is only by looking closely at a country or region's history that we can unravel the roots of these modern-day issues, unpeel the layers, and adopt genuine solutions. We touched on Ukraine's troubled history in chapter 2, but now let's look a little closer to see the cause and effects more clearly.

Roots of Fatherlessness in Ukraine

To begin, Ukraine has a history of dictatorships that forced citizens to be subservient and impotent.[1] Early twentieth-century theorists Karl Marx and Friedrich Engles idealized a strict socialist society and believed that families should be dissolved and couples should exist essentially only for procreation. The State should provide collective services to feed, do laundry, and provide childcare. As a result, living conditions became deplorable, and it cost the State beyond what it could sustain.

Stalin reinstated the family as a unit believing that mothers should stay at home and provide for their children but continued to keep fathers divided and excluded. This intentional disruption of the family unit is a tactic to maintain control. Stalin believed if a leader controlled the family politically, the entire population would be controlled.

His idea that a stable family meant one dependent on the state was useful during the years of The Great Terror—mass purges that took place in the mid-thirties. The purges touched each household in the Soviet Union. Stalin turned family against family and even family members against each other. As described in Solzhenitsyn's *The Gulag Archipelago*:

> The widespread use of communal apartments facilitated government oppression. Initially designed to address a severe housing crisis, the apartments turned into 'a means of extending the state's powers of surveillance into the private spaces of the family home.' Families could monitor one another, reporting any hint of disloyalty. Spouses and children could be sent away after an arrest or an execution. The age of criminal responsibility was lowered to twelve in order to reinforce pressure on adults to cooperate with interrogators and spare their children. A wife was expected to divorce her arrested husband.[2]

Stalin's philosophy essentially did three things to men under socialism.

- Took away their role as fathers
- Took away their role as husbands
- Took away their role as leaders within their household

The father was eliminated from any parenting responsibility beyond procreation and therefore effectively eliminated from involvement with the family.

Instead, they were out working, often far from home, finding other female relationships and not having a hand at all in working with their own children. They were conditioned into a culture of father absence.

Remember the circle Sasha drew on the board for the social worker students? They had been led to believe that the father was outside of and separate from the family. Not at all the model of family that humans need to develop, or that society needs to thrive.

Making Positive Change in Ukraine

Prior to beginning our ministry in Ukraine, we knew we needed a better understanding of the specific issues they faced—we couldn't assume their issues would be the same as what we face in the United States. In order to address Ukraine's specific cultural and political influences, we conducted extensive research and commissioned a professional assessment of the current state of the nation. From here, we could target strategies to help them reclaim their fathers and their families.

It begins with education. Much that happened during the seventy-year Communist rule in Ukraine had been written out of the history books and only recently exposed to modern day Ukrainians. This was something that Sasha would highlight for our audiences during our presentations and begin to pull back the curtain on how the events specifically targeted and damaged the father role within families.

But even with the opportunity to make changes, many lost hope that it could ever change. On one occasion while in Ukraine, Chuck and I concluded a meeting with some high-ranking officials and promptly came upon a group of sixty social workers meeting in the same building. Our escort recognized the connection of our shared mission and led us in.

The group was all women, and they invited us to share about our work helping men understand their roles as fathers and husbands. And yet as we did, they immediately voiced objections. From their experience, what we proposed absolutely would not work. Their society had moved so far from the two-parent model it was beyond saving. Families, including these women, had known no other life. It was hopeless.

All we could say was that we understood the enormous task and would not expect it to happen fast or easily. It would have to start by taking baby steps, one at a time. We told them we were seeing it work in literally thousands of families in their own country. In fact, we had just finished meeting with government officials to which the response was one of amazement and a request to please help them. We encouraged the group of social workers to keep the faith and keep doing their powerful work.

Interestingly, the original invitation to National Center for Fathering to come and help with fathering did not come from Ukraine but from post-Communist Russia. Two university professors from Moscow had read Ken Canfield's book *The Seven Secrets of Effective Fathers* in the early 1990s and wanted someone from Ken's ministry in Kansas City to come to help them. This led to a team traveling over in 1998 to explore the possibilities.

But the cultural influence of communism, of looking over their collective shoulders to see who might be watching them, was still too strong in Russia to allow for the change that was needed. Instead, the organization found their way to Ukraine where the communities and culture were more open and receptive to the material. And so change was possible.

The work began in Kyiv after the 1998 trip, with teams traveling twice a year for two weeks at a time. The work desperately needed a Ukrainian leader, and in 2002, Sasha Marchenko was recommended as a likely candidate. He felt led to accept the position even though the promise of funds for ministry and salary were slim. The US dollars went further than Ukrainian hryvnia and made it possible, along with Sasha's utter devotion to his calling, for him and his family to scrape by.

Volunteers were recruited, an oversight board was selected, seminars were set up all over Ukraine, and thousands of men and families were impacted by the National Center for Fatherhood of Ukraine each year. In 2013, the organization was completely handed over to the Ukrainian leadership without our oversight.

While their initial response to this hand-off was shock, it was the release they needed to take ownership, and they began to flourish as never before. They have since instituted an annual Father's Day celebration in five Oblisks (like counties) with the encouragement and endorsement of the government of Ukraine, and a new executive director has been named to free up Sasha for program and fund development.[3]

History of Fatherlessness in the United States

Now let's look closer to home and our own history of fatherlessness. The National Center for Fathering commissioned a professional assessment of the state of fatherlessness in the United States as well. Shockingly, despite Ukraine's extreme historical circumstances of communism, war, and dictatorship, the outcomes of fatherlessness in the United States are exactly the same.

The first major influence to the state of fatherlessness in the United States and around the world was the Industrial Revolution, which occurred gradually from 1760 to 1840. This caused a major shift in the way families lived as farmers left the countryside and moved into the city to engage in factory work. Rather than working at home on their farms, where family and work were integrated, factory work separated fathers from their families. The second Industrial Revolution took place from 1870 to 1914, the beginning of World War I, and led to even more upheaval and separation of the family.

World War I and World War II also contributed to men being taken away from their families, at least for a period of time to fight, if not forever through death. The level of industrial production that the country had reached by World War II and sought to maintain as well as grow during wartime put women to work en masse to fill in for the absent male workers. Now both fathers and mothers were increasingly absent from the home, and a shift in lifestyle was required.

To be clear, this is not a criticism of women going to work, but rather an observation that it led to a change in the family structure, drawing both men and women out of the traditional roles of father and mother and the nuclear family.

More recent factors to change the historical family structure have been the rise of single-parent families, same-sex parent families, and an increase in the number of unwed mothers. The assessment cited all of these changes as having a negative impact on the majority of children, due in large part to the continued absence of the father, or the balance of the father and the mother role that shapes a child's foundation and identity.

As stated in chapters 6 and 7, it is these roles that are most significant in generating an individual's positive identity. Such rapid changes to family structure without awareness of the impact when one of the parental roles is missing has led, in large part, to the cycles of anger and absence that we have now. Mindful parenting can ensure these roles are filled in the child's life, regardless of the household structure.

Supporting Father Presence in the United States

Prenatal and neonatal parenting programs. The best solutions start early in life, so DadsFirst makes visits to public schools, major corporations, state universities, and hospitals to work with first-time dads. I have heard many young men say they are afraid of becoming a father because they do not know how to be one or are afraid of the commitment. I believe most of those men come from families where the father did not model or create a healthy atmosphere of family love and support where family is enjoyed and encouraged. They are understandably running from the unknown and from bad experiences.

Young men from a more healthy family background know there are resources to learn about fathering including "on-the-job" training and good spousal and family/friend support networks. Besides the pregnant couple learning together in our prenatal program, soon-to-be dads often opt to take our six-week crash course on becoming a father.

School programs. In working with a former Minneapolis Superintendent of schools, he assured us that unless a child has a father, grandfather, or father role in their life when they come to us for kindergarten, they are already lost to us.

All our work is designed to help others understand that fathering is the heart and soul of relationships and to experience greater, lasting, positive changes in families, primarily through reconciliation with one's father. In one urban community, we created a program that served the specific needs of Black dads of preschool kids.

Another outstanding organization developed a school program called Watch D.O.G.S., or Dads of Great Students, which has been implemented in over 6,500 schools across the US with amazing results. Google it and check it out. It works!

Inmate programs. DadsFirst works directly with the Minnesota prison system to specifically address father issues. The inmates were asked to identify the goals they would like as a result of their work with us on this topic.

Here are the top 15 goals that the inmates shared:

1. Learn how to resolve resentment towards my father.

2. Learn the basics of being a father/being a better father.

3. Learn how to connect and/or stay connected with my children while I'm in prison.

4. Learn how to talk to my kids about the tough questions while in prison, including sex.

5. Learn how to deal with my son or daughter's anger over my being in prison.

6. Discuss resources available regarding my child support responsibilities and rights.

7. Learn how to be better at taking responsibility for myself and teaching responsibility to my kids.

8. Discuss the transition back into my family and my community.

9. Discuss the aspects of a relationship with my child's mother in order to have a relationship with my children.

10. Discuss a father's parental rights and/or where to get legal help.

11. Learn how to be more productive and to avoid a criminal mindset.

12. Learn how to be a model citizen.

13. Learn how to have a relationship with my own father.

14. Learn how to be a God-glorifying father.

15. Learn how our relationship with our earthly father affects our relationship with our heavenly father.

Having just listed those things, it is important to note that most inmates never get the opportunity to look into these topics, and most incarcerated parents never get a single visit from their children.

It's also significant to note that children who do not visit their parents in prison perpetuate the generational problems. These children rarely live full-time with their fathers before they went to prison. In some cases, mothers or other caregivers discourage or actively obstruct the children's contact with incarcerated fathers. But this is actually more harmful to both the child and the father and perpetuates the generational cycle of fatherlessness.

Imagine if men and fathers who are not in prison would have the same goals and desires, how that would impact their business and their home life.

Just the Beginning

Even though the histories of Ukraine and the United States are very different, the outcome and statistics are the same. The damage of absence and neglect spread beyond the wounded individual, across generations and sects of society, until our entire culture is tainted with misogyny and misandry.

What is the solution?

The ministries and programs mentioned in this chapter are noble beginnings. But in truth, they are not enough. They are not yet widespread or commonplace. They are unique. To turn the tide on the pandemic-sized problem of father absence, we need a solution of equal or greater impact.

Like Ukraine, we need support at the highest level—we need leaders and influencers to take action in their sphere of influence. But we need something else even more. We need to forgive our fathers.

Part III

The Cure for Uninvolvement

Chapter 19

The Power of Reconciliation

"To forgive is to set the prisoner free, and then discover the prisoner was you."

—ANONYMOUS

In a church in western Ukraine, we were treated to a light breakfast, and then Sasha started off the first session for that day's seminar.

"Good morning, men," he said. "Last night we challenged you to consider our topic of reconciliation and to make a plan to do something about it. This morning, we want to hear from any of you who made some progress."

"I want to be first. I cannot be silent." To our surprise, it was our translator, Yuri, speaking.

I say surprised because, while an excellent translator, he also seemed a bit removed from the content the evening before, as though he was just doing his job as an outsider.

At Sasha's invitation, Yuri immediately headed for the microphone. He wasn't going to wait to be called on. He was an energetic young man, but now he was obviously a bit nervous, even on the edge of tears. We didn't know what to expect from his mix of emotions.

"I was moved by what I heard last night," he began, "and felt compelled to talk to my father. We haven't talked in a few years and never were real close. He was always busy working or out with his friends and never showed any interest in me as a child or while I was growing up. I always wanted to know him and to be with him, but as I grew up I forgot about it. Until last night. The meeting made me think and remember things."

He paused, and we could see in his eyes that he was still remembering and evaluating his thoughts.

"Once, when I was ten years old, he took me fishing. Otherwise we have never talked or done things together. I've always sensed this hole in my heart that I could not explain until last night's teaching. I went home determined to call him, but I was afraid. I sat by the phone trying to make myself pick it up and call him, but I could not. I finally decided to put it off and go to bed when the phone rang and made me jump because it startled me. It was quite late by then, and I answered curiously, 'Hello?'"

"'Hello, son.' It was my father! I couldn't believe it. I figured something bad must have happened and he had to contact the family.

"What is it, Papa? What's wrong?"

"'Son, I've been thinking a lot about you as my son and about me as your father. I want to tell you how sorry I am for not being there for you and that I love you. Would you please forgive me?'"

By now, Yuri was having a hard time talking as his emotions were overcoming him. Most of the men were overcome with tears, as well.

"I about fell off my chair. I couldn't believe it." He sobbed. "I said yes and asked him to forgive me, too. We were both in tears and so happy. I didn't know what had caused him to call me at the same time I wanted to call him—and almost didn't call. We made a time to get together to talk some more. I am crying, but I am so happy."

The room erupted in cheers and applause.

It was the first of several similar stories that morning. They were great testimonies of bringing a dark and hurtful experience in their lives into the light, exposing the evil behind it, and turning it into good. Not everyone had a story to tell that night—or ever—but it was encouraging to see reconciliation in action.

What Is Reconciliation?

All of us fail to some extent in our role as fathers. That's true for our fathers, too, and their fathers before them. How we deal with that failure is more important than the failure itself. Jazz great Miles Davis once said, "It's not the note you play that's the wrong note, it's the note you play afterwards that makes it right or wrong." Author Richard Rohr makes this more pertinent to reconciliation with his comment, "If we do not transform our pain, we will most assuredly transmit it."[1]

So often, we see the past as the past and move on without dealing with it. Unfortunately, not dealing with it makes it more likely to be repeated.

In our DadsFirst lessons, we say, "How we deal with the hurt and wounds of our own father's failures determines our ability to be good fathers (or mothers) to our children." That is an important statement. I certainly wasn't aware of it at all as a young father, and in my observation, few men are. Since we all have father wounds, and since dealing with the past is so essential for future success, we all need to face those relationships to bring healing. But how? There is help. Along with the realization and motivation that we are developing, we also need to learn basic techniques and skills. So let's begin.

Reconciliation means:

- To bring together what was once apart
- To heal something that was broken.
- To settle a relationship

The process of restoring relationships through forgiveness and understanding is what reconciliation is all about. It's important to realize that reconciliation is not about restoring things back to what they once were. We can restore an old house or old car to what it once was, but we can't do that with relationships. We might think we want the former things back based on old, false memories, but it will never happen. Good or bad, things will never be like they used to be. The relationship has been broken, and reconciliation is about bringing them back together again, albeit in a new way.

Therefore, in relationships, restoration is about looking to the future to develop a new relationship based on what we want and hope to be. With this viewpoint, the journey can become hopeful and expectant rather than fearful and resisted.

I believe people genuinely want to have a good relationship with other people. They want to *restore and heal* relationships. They want to have *understanding.* It's just that they don't know how, don't want to go through the hurt and the pain or the vulnerability required to bring understanding and to either give or receive forgiveness. It requires facing our mistakes and making changes. Pride and the need to be right might be the biggest obstacles—after all, who wants to admit they were wrong?

We all know through experience that reconciliation is basic to our relationships and happiness—but still we resist it. Reconciliation is a cornerstone goal of most all philosophies and principles of human compatibility. For example, there is a Biblical passage that underscores how significant reconciliation is and makes it a core message of the whole Christian faith. It says "God...settled the relationship between us and him, and then called us to settle our relationships with each other."[2] That is our job—to be reconciled with one another.

Reconciling Self-Worth in Ukraine

When talking to classes of high school seniors, I took the lead to address the concept of self-worth. After years of being immersed in communist culture that diminishes the individual in deference to the value of the State, citizens had been taught that they need to be subservient and meek, and that they have no real individual value. Even if they have standout talents, they are not to promote them, simply to use them but be meek about it. This culture is hard to change, and as a result, teachers and parents regularly put young people down and squash their initiative. They know this about themselves and that it is a national issue.

I began by drawing an image of a large glass bottle on the blackboard. It was rough and got plenty of laughs when I explained what it was. I filled it in with small circles to represent marbles.

"This bottle represents your bank of self-worth. When someone compliments how you look or what you say, it adds more marbles to your bank."

I drew a few more.

"When they put you down or are unkind to you, it withdraws marbles."

I erased some.

"If you are a person with a large bank account and someone causes marbles to be withdrawn, it doesn't hurt much. You still have many left. But if you have very few marbles to begin with, the same bad comment can leave you bankrupt or close to it."

I emptied the bottle.

"If our bank account is low, we tend to avoid people and circumstances that may bankrupt us, such as certain friends, our parents, or going to school. We need to be aware of our own bank accounts, but the best way to do this is to be aware of the accounts of those around you. What you say may not be a big deal to you, but it may cause the other person to go bankrupt. You know what that feels like, and it's not good.

"When we encourage someone, it builds them up for good, not for a big head or a heart of pride. The world is a hard place, and we need all the encouragement we can get. Our goal ought to be to fill the bank accounts of those around us so that they end each day with more self-esteem than they had at the beginning. Everyone needs this, and everyone needs to help with this. Not just students, but teachers, custodians, bus drivers, parents, siblings, everyone.

"And even though the society and our circumstances may promote poor self-esteem, we have learned that, surprisingly, the father is the most important person in our lives for giving us our identity, sense of confidence, and self-worth. That's why what we are telling you today is so important."

Once again, understanding and agreement was evident on their faces. Teachers, in particular, seemed moved and even embarrassed of themselves. This was a big deal.

Words Every Father Needs to Say

I have heard several speakers on this subject of fathering ask audiences of men, "How many of you ever had your father actually say out loud to you, 'I love you?'" They might get four or five hands out of a hundred in the room. Considering times had changed, I thought I would try it, too, just to see what the response would be. I asked the question at several events to men, most of whom were in their twenties to forties, with a few older men mixed in. The responses were the same—about 5 percent raised their hands. As I went through the topic, I also got a lot of tears. The hurt—the wound—was obvious.

Saying *I love you* is part of the process of being able to accept ourselves for who we are. It is a part of accepting our identity and of being blessed, not for what we do but for who we are. We have a wonderful model for this in the Bible in the story of Jesus' baptism by John the Baptist. This model was first introduced to me by the honorable Al Quie, former governor of the State of Minnesota.

There was a voice that came from heaven. The voice was God's, and it said, "You are my son, whom I love. I am very proud of you."[3] This example contains three significant elements that every father ought to say to his children.

First is a statement of belonging: "You are my son."

Hearing that means, "I belong to someone."

Each of us needs to hear that from our fathers. Girls long to hear, "You are my daughter," too.

Even with dad around all the time, that message doesn't usually get said. In reality, every one of us has experienced or will experience some degree of abandonment by our father or someone else in authority. Because of the significance of the relationship, the act of not being chosen creates an even deeper desire to hear our father call our name. This desire doesn't stop at childhood. Remember, Jesus was about thirty years old at that time.

Second is a statement of acceptance: "I love you."

Those three words counter abandonment. We each need to hear that there is someone who cares. I need to hear it from anyone, but especially from my dad. Even if we are estranged and I say I hate my father, deep down I wish we were best buds and that he would say to me, "I love you." This is a broad generalization, but I believe it applies to everyone who has a father.

The third is a statement of unconditional love: "I am very proud of you."

This speaks to our sense of self-worth and personal value by countering the messages of shame we each receive in our lives. Shame yells, "You are not worthwhile. I am not choosing you." If dad is at work too much, that's the message we hear: "I choose work instead of you."

This third statement counters with the message from dad, the one designed to be our hero in life, "I choose you, and you are mine." Hearing it, we breathe a sigh of relief. It is a balm to our hearts.

At what time in Jesus' life did he hear those words of unconditional love? At the beginning of his ministry. What that tells me is that Jesus did not have to go out and prove himself in order to be loved and accepted. His father loved him and *then* sent him out. Jesus knew who he was and *whose* he was. Every son and daughter needs to hear this blessing—and often. It is a message of confidence in who we are.

I have one more thing to say about this meaningful story at the baptism: All the people around heard the voice of the father giving his son this awesome blessing. Dads, don't be shy or passive about this. Let everyone know how you feel. Your kids will be doubly blessed when they see how strongly you mean it and how proud you are.

Keep saying it when your kids are grown, too—just imagine the impact of employees hearing their boss telling his sons and daughters that he loves them.

Putting It Off

Forgiving your father should not be put off. We as men are very good at procrastinating and putting off these difficult relationship things. We will often say "I don't have time." "I'm busy." "He's too far away." "He's dead." "He's too angry." "He doesn't deserve it." "I hate him and can't bring myself to do it."

We can come up with all kinds of excuses. And that's what they are—nothing more than excuses. We really do have all the time in the world for reconciliation, because again, that's why we are here—for relationships.

"What if I'm so wounded that I can't face him yet? I know I will someday, but can I put it off for now?" Here is a personal example of how that works. It is not a father-son story, but an example of needing time to process the wound:

I had an incident with a supervisor, years ago. I never found out what prompted him to turn it into such a major conflict, but from my perspective, he had "gotten rid of" several other employees in a similar way. He was even accusing me of doing things I most certainly didn't do. As a result, I went into a depression, which left me even more vulnerable to attack. I didn't realize this until I was coming out of it several months after leaving the company.

When attacked, I couldn't think due to the depression, and I responded by lashing out and making inappropriate comments to defend myself. I was wounded, and for several years, even the thought of stepping foot in the place made me nauseated. I knew that one day I would be able to forgive the man, but for the time being I was unable to face him. The pain needed to subside first.

Finally, healing began to set in, and about five years later I was able to call him up and ask if he would meet me for coffee. I assumed he was expecting at least a dialogue about our time of conflict if not outright blame. I started by saying, "I did not come here to talk about what happened between us or to blame or to make excuses. I only want to say that there were times I responded inappropriately to what was being said or done, and for that I want to ask your forgiveness." That was the only thing I felt bad about, so it was the only thing I needed to apologize for. He about dropped his coffee cup, but recovered enough to say, "Of course. I forgive you, and would you please forgive me?"

His was less specific and was prompted by my request, but we both knew it covered a lot and was sincere. The point is, it took time for me to be ready for forgiveness and reconciliation—during which time, I never let go of the possibility that we could come to this conclusion.

The Other Side of the Equation: Asking for Forgiveness

What? Ask for forgiveness? Admit I was wrong?! Asking for forgiveness seems to violate my personal right. It challenges my need to be right even when I know I am wrong!

What will it take to bring us to the place of asking for forgiveness? First, humility. Webster's dictionary defines humility as "freedom from pride or arrogance." If you think that's hard for you, imagine how hard it is for your father. Second, it will take us remembering the benefits of going through the pain of asking and of getting to the unspeakable joy of being reconciled. Third, knowing from experience how much you dislike admitting that you are wrong becomes its own deterrent to words and behavior that can get you into trouble in the first place.

Did you notice the twist in that last story? I had to forgive the man in my own heart, but then I felt led to turn it around and ask him to forgive me. That surprised even me at the time, but it was the right thing to do. Why?

First, it completely eliminated any blame or accusation or defense of my position. I'm sure he expected that, but when it didn't come, he didn't have to be in a defensive posture either.

Second, as the saying goes, "It takes two to tango." It demonstrated my acceptance of the fact that conflict is never one-sided. No one is ever without blame. He heard me admit to being wrong, and it gave him permission to do the same.

Third, it created an atmosphere of moving toward the other person, with a genuine interest to reconcile.

The Likely Outcome: How It Usually Works

Here's what I know from experience about giving and receiving forgiveness. Forgiving someone immediately takes away all the power that the offense held. It is no longer possible to hold it over the head of the other person.

In this case, the mutual forgiveness also brought immediate reconciliation. We actually became good friends again and were able to bless one another, and we never brought up the details of the fallout, nor did we want to. Not that there aren't times to revisit conflict in order to learn and grow from them from a position of respect and understanding rather than the need to be right. All the angst I had felt for those years was released and replaced by a peace and calm. Most likely my supervisor had no idea I had been struggling as much as I had. It was only impacting me and my poor wife. As I consider it, he might have been carrying a weight from our fallout, as well, I don't know. Now it was done and gone, and I was able to breathe and move on.

The moral of the story is twofold.

First, allow time for healing, but don't use that as an excuse to put it off too long or forever. The gravity of the offense will be part of dictating how long it will take.

Second, start by asking for forgiveness. No one will see it coming, and it works. In any case, you are in control of your own choices in this regard, so act appropriately throughout the process of setting yourself and the other party free.

Conflict and Resolution

Everywhere we turn, everywhere we look, we see situations of difficulties, conflicts, and hurts between fathers and children, both as children and as adults. We see them on TV shows, in movies and books, and at home, work, and church—they're everywhere. Most of the time, we recognize the problems and even know what to do to fix them and the other person. However, when it comes to our own lives, we get into the same troubles and either don't recognize the issues or don't know what to do about them. When I hold a mirror up to people in trouble, or one is held up to me, it's as if we don't recognize ourselves. We don't see how blind, silly, stupid, awful, mean, ignorant, arrogant, selfish, cruel, hateful, even dumb we are being. It's all part of the issue of being self-protecting, right, and passive about life—caught in the matrix of life, numb to the reality of one's attitude and behavior.

These avoidance tactics are the same for any conflict that arises. I usually ask my clients how they deal with conflict with family, friends, and associates. The most common answer is, "I avoid it. Eventually, it goes away."

My response sounds like Dr. Phil: "So how's that working out for you?"

When being honest, the client realizes it's only an attempt to escape and never heals the hurt, bitterness, injustice, and resentment. Yes, all those words describe what happens with conflict avoidance. In fact, here are a few more that I have observed: contempt, rage, hatred, betrayal, revenge, and anger. That list ought to be enough to make us eager to resolve all conflict.

When told we must forgive and reconcile with someone, our first reaction is to find anything else to do but that. Hitting my thumb with a hammer might even sound like a good alternative. Everything inside us yells, "Conflict! Avoid! You don't want to go there." Facing the need to reconcile with one's father is like that conflict avoidance.

Letting Go

I have talked with people who have held grudges for most of their lives. They might hold them against their fathers, other family members, or previous employees.

I remember a woman coming to me during a break where I'd been speaking at a conference on conflict resolution. Once again, it's a business setting, but it demonstrates how this happens with fathers, too.

The woman was in her fifties. She told me what had happened at her previous job where she had been let go. She sincerely believed the company made a mistake and could not function well without her. She also believed the company was struggling in her absence and was regretting their decision. If only she could communicate with them, she knew she could show them the folly of their decision and they would hire her back. I asked her how long ago this had happened, and she admitted it had been quite a few years. "What!?" you might think, but the reality is that many people have this response, particularly if they had been in the business for a long time and felt their role mattered.

It is easy for otherwise sane and rational employees to become deluded by circumstances that are not approached with direct and open dialogue. This woman was carrying bitterness about an action that was impacting her mind, body, and ability to move on with her life. I asked her how she knew that people at the business were regretting this decision.

She jumped right in, "Oh, they have to be struggling because I was such a crucial piece in their operation. I was the go-to person for everything. No one knew more about the company than I did." She assumed that they were thinking about it all the time, carrying around bad feelings of guilt and struggling with their mistake of letting her go.

Since she had come to me asking for my input, I first explained the difference of perspective that a person in leadership has from that of an employee and how that affects decisions. The leader has more information and must see the big picture. The employee sees only their realm of influence. With that in mind, I asked if I could be frank with her, and she agreed. I said, "This might be hard to hear, but I believe the reality is that they haven't thought about it once since you left. The only one thinking about it is you, and it has trapped you in anger and bitterness and kept you from moving on."

Immediately, I saw several things reflected in her expression: hurt, embarrassment, and understanding. It hurt to be told her past role didn't matter to them. She was embarrassed that she was the only one still thinking about it and had been her own jailer in this prison of bitterness. Finally, with understanding came the knowledge that she needed to move on. Time had not healed her resentment and had only made the bitterness worse. Her story showed that if we don't deal past painful relationships, they will only get worse.

Chapter 20

Reconciliation in Individuals

"Without forgiveness, without reconciliation, we have no future."

—DESMOND TUTU

I have come across many family businesses that are experiencing wonderful relationships. Sure, there are times of trouble and conflict, but they have found ways to deal with those difficulties when they come. They have prepared and put strategies in place for those times. There is an atmosphere of congeniality and understanding that pervades the relationships so that conflicts are seen simply as nuisances that can and will be solved or as important lessons to be learned.

There are so many more, however, that never get to that place. The constant power struggles and the need to be right overshadow the daily life of the business and its members. When I get to know the individuals in these dysfunctional families, the overriding observation is that the attitudes and behaviors have been going on for generations. They have been inherited, modeled, and passed on, and will likely continue to be for generations to come. The anger and loathing simmering beneath the surface of daily life is toxic. It is a tragedy and feels hopeless to change. They think it is because of the activities and actions from the other person or people that they can list off. In reality, it is deeper than that. The animosity exists in the heart. Art Rouner describes it this way:

> Love lives in the heart. When love is betrayed, when
> trust is ravaged, when friendship sours, or when a
> bond of human friendship is broken, it is the heart
> that lies wounded. It is the heart that even physically
> feels 'broken.' And when that happens, life itself
> is imperiled...the heart of a [business or family] is
> terrorized. Fear lies everywhere. Every [person] is
> affected. No one escapes.[1]

There is not an easy fix, but it can happen.

The first requirement is to recognize and admit that conflict and division exist. This is a huge step of humility, not an easy thing for most of us. We have a well-developed sense of pride, right or wrong.

The second is to want to do something about it to bring about change.

And *the third* is to take action.

The action that is required is reconciliation between those who are caught in the web of the struggle. While reconciliation is a necessary step for conflicts that exist between any two individuals, the conflict is often a result of an unresolved conflict between individuals and their own fathers. In other words, the father relationship is central to all other relationships. Resolving conflict in that relationship raises up a whole inner change in one's heart toward others. Having forgiven one's father, a heart of peace begins to mature—one of greater understanding, acceptance, and love. It's amazing to see this work over and over. It is a fundamental step in conflict resolution.

The linchpin in this whole sequence is the father-child relationship. It is the grassroots of it all. The father is the one most responsible for the future success, or lack thereof, of his sons and daughters. How he deals with the hurt of his own father's failures determines his ability to be a good parent to his children!

The point is, every one of us has a father, and every one of us has a father wound. I have had men say to me defensively, "I had a great father and wonderful relationship with him. I don't have a father wound, and it sounds like you want me to go on a witch hunt to find one."

I say, "Congratulations, you are fortunate indeed to have a wound so small you don't recognize it."

The father wound varies from person to person and can be difficult to see depending on one's perspective. Look at it this way: the father wound is the difference between what your dad is able to give you and your potential as the father you were created to be. With some, it may be very minor due to a good earthly father influence. In such cases, it is not necessary to try to go digging up issues that may not exist in order to find the wounding. Others have a huge father wound and yet do amazingly well in spite of it, usually due to a strong relationship with the one who created them. They identify with God the father for great fathering instincts.

However, thinking this through, even a small wound will benefit by evaluating and understanding this complete topic, and intentionally extending good fathering as a benefit to others and to future generations. It helps to eliminate blind spots, and the reality is, we can all improve. It is largely a matter of comparisons.

The bigger the wound, the easier it is to see and feel. The small ones go unrecognized and undealt with. They may be inconsequential, but likely not.

We all need to consider going through this process of reconciliation to resolve and heal a relationship that is holding us back from becoming who we are capable of becoming, from moving forward in the conflicts we have with others. That is the power of the father role and of the reconciliation process: you have been walking in your father's footsteps whether you realize it or not.

It calls to mind a story that often crept into my mind as a young father myself.

> A father in his late twenties was having difficulties
> from various pressures at work and home. He had

a wonderful wife and a seven-year-old son, but his struggles were forcing him to walk across the field each evening to the tavern to escape. One dark wintry evening as he trudged through the deep snow, he sensed someone behind him and stopped to take a look. There was his young son, struggling to put his feet into the holes his dad's feet had made in the snow. "Keep going dad," the boy yelled. "I'm following in your footsteps."

The words shot like an arrow into the dad's heart. He immediately recognized the deeper meaning of his son's words and the poor model he was becoming as a dad. He lovingly picked up his son, and headed home to confront his own behavior.

Steps to Restore and Heal a Healthy Relationship

There is no one magic method for resolving your relationship with your father, and it is a process over time. The methods are many and varied. However, in working with many individuals in our fathering ministry and clients, I use the following steps outlined by author Ken Canfield.[2] The process ought to include some or all of these five elements:

1. Meet to exchange your thoughts.

Don't leave it to the father to initiate reconciliation. While some will, it is unlikely that most fathers will do this. The son or daughter needs to take the initiative. You may choose to call your dad, drop in and see him, or make a pot of coffee and talk. The important thing is to take the initiative and do it.

If your father has died, it is not an excuse. Write a Dear Dad letter and read it to him at his graveside. If he is gone and unavailable, write your letter and then put it away or even destroy it if you choose. It works because the value of forgiveness and reconciliation is for you first, then for others. This is a very important point that most of us do not recognize. Going through the exercise will bring healing and release for you as you work through the process.

Because we use this exercise often, we have copies of dozens of letters we have kept, many from men who never even knew their fathers. Their words are packed with emotion, and some are moved to healing and forgiveness if they are at that place in their own understanding—others are moved to rage if they aren't yet at that stage. The point is, even without knowing their fathers, they were inextricably linked to them.

Often, when a person wants to move toward forgiveness and reconciliation, the other person is not at the same place, making it difficult to even approach the subject. If they aren't ready, they are less likely to accept and respond positively. Who wants to approach that? Therefore, it's important to make the effort, and the key is to prepare for it ahead of time. If possible, it's also important to prepare the other person so as to diminish further conflict or devolve into a shouting match.

Preparing the other person may be as basic as letting them know you want to meet to talk: "Dad, I have some things to talk with you about and would like to meet one-to-one over a cup of coffee. Would you be up for that sometime soon?" Also, be prepared for a *no*, or at least a skeptical response. Fathers can feel quite threatened by sons and daughters who "want to talk."

Let's revisit my client Don, from chapter 1, as a good example of this step in the process.

After some time, Don finally agreed to the idea of writing the Dear Dad letter. Remember, Don hated their relationship. He didn't know how to start, and all the venom he had was getting in the way. This happens with most men, and we suggest they just start writing. It's okay to practice over several tries to get the letter they want to use.

Don's first letter was accusatory and blaming—a one-sided shouting match on paper. It was a diatribe, blaming and accusing his dad of all the wrong he had done.

I said, "Don, I want you to listen to me read this to you as if I were you and you were your dad." I wanted him to hear it from another perspective. The message got through, and he continued to write several versions, each one moving closer to forgiveness and reconciliation.

Finally, Don had an *aha!* moment that changed his whole perspective. It, too, is a common revelation. I said, "Don, do you know what your father's father was like?"

"He was just like my dad," he said. "I couldn't stand being around him either. My dad hated him, too."

That's when the revelation sank in.

Don's dad wasn't trying to be mad at or cruel to him—he was simply acting out what he learned from his own father. Once Don understood this, his heart melted.

He had compassion and was able to sincerely forgive his father and begin to move towards him to build a right relationship. His next versions of the letter improved drastically.

2. Express your feelings.

Think this through ahead of time, and even practice having the conversation. If your talks always turn into arguments, there is other work to do first, as with step 1 above. This is not a time to blame, accuse, or be right. To get the conversation going, you might ask, "What was your childhood like? Tell me about your friends, your school, your room. What hobbies did you have?"

When Don finally got to the place of having a real conversation with his father, he asked him, "What was your father like?" It was something his dad had put out of his mind, but with prompting, he really opened up. He told about all the difficulties and how hard it was to be around his dad.

Don's only response was, "I know what you mean, my father was just the same."

His dad got the point.

This is a time to express how you felt or were impacted by your lives together. Tell about the hard times as matters of fact and how you were impacted by them. That may take some explaining. He may try to say you aren't right, that it's not what happened, or that he disagrees. It will help to set up the conversation by saying something like, "Dad, keep in mind I might be right or wrong, good or bad, but I am saying these things from my perspective. This is how I saw it, felt it and interpreted it. I'm not trying to change the past, I'm just telling it from my point of view." Your feelings are your feelings, and they cannot be argued against. Regardless of how your father may view what happened, he cannot argue with how you were impacted.

When you express your feelings toward your father, be careful and prepared with the right words and attitude, not a vomiting of emotions and accusations. This is critical. In your preparation, always ask yourself, "What do I want for me, and what don't I want for me?" and "What do I want for my father and what don't I want for him?" For example, what you might want is to say your piece without being interrupted. What you don't want is to be misunderstood. You might want your father to be encouraged and to understand. You might not want for him to be angry and defensive.

Thinking through these ideas ahead of time will help to choose your words going into the conversation. The entire process of seeking to build a new relationship with your father must always be bathed in honor and respect for the office of father, if not for the man himself.

3. Confess your faults.

Guess what? Not only is your father not perfect, you aren't perfect either. The word *responsible* means "able to respond." As the father, he may have been responsible for how he treated you, but especially now as an adult, you are responsible for how you respond. Think through ways in which you were at fault, ways in which you may have contributed to the division. This takes a great deal of humility. It takes a real man or woman to come to the point of admitting and confessing wrongs done.

Confess your faults and own your actions without rationalizing or making excuses. Put aside your need to be right, your self-justification, and hiding from your strengths. You can do it. Where you have dishonored your father, confess that to him.

One definition of the word "reconcile" reads: "to remove all enmity and leave no impediment to unity and peace."

I have discovered that, when confessing and asking for forgiveness. once it is given, the power of one person to hold the offense over the other person is suddenly gone. It may not erase all the consequences of the offense, but if a person forgives you of an offense, they cannot hold it against you anymore. That's the wonderful result of shining the light into the dark areas of bad relationships. That's not to mean we're getting away with something—it means we're being healed and forgiven. That's great joy and freedom!

4. Forgive your father.

Confession is owning your part, and forgiveness comes next. Forgiving your father is the other response you are able to do. This may seem more impossible and frightening than confessing, but it is doable and necessary.

You may have deep wounds inflicted by the men who were entrusted with your care—first and foremost, your father. You might say, "Forgive him? No way! He doesn't deserve it and hasn't changed. I'll never forgive him for the way he treated me (or my mother)." Remember that this whole process is about you and your healing first of all, and then the relationship.

Understand that, in forgiving your father, you are not condoning his behavior and pretending like nothing happened. Forgiveness faces the facts *with* all their pain, and then decides on purpose not to hold these actions against him. Remember again, the overall goal is to establish a new relationship,

Your forgiveness is not dependent on your father's repentance or response. He may be unwilling or unable to accept your forgiveness. This does not mean you cannot forgive him. Forgiveness is something you do on your own initiative with or without his cooperation.

If your sincere aim is to make peace with your father and to move on in a life of joyful wholeness, you have no choice but to forgive him. If you don't move on to this step with the goal of a new relationship with your father, you are likely to be left feeling stung by regret or anger and will pass the broken pieces and attitude of unforgiveness on to the next generation.

You may have to allow yourself some time to truly forgive your father. It may not happen in one face-to-face meeting. It may take many meetings with your dad to forgive him. Give yourself some space, but at the same time, commit to the discipline of forgiveness.

5. Commit to a new relationship.

Taking each of these steps will settle your emotions and open the door for a new relationship with your father. You must commit yourself to such a direction. "Dad, I know some things have not been very good between us, but with the years that you and I have left together, I'm going to do my part to make things better. I'll always be your son, and you'll always be my father." Now is the time to say, "Dad, I love you."

Taking these steps will serve as a rite of passage from being the son or daughter to being the father or mother that you choose to be. You have grasped the baton of family leadership. The next leg of the race is yours to run. These steps can apply to other conflicted relationships once the father wound is dealt with.

Now I'll ask you what I ask everyone in DadsFirst courses: If this material has changed your way of thinking concerning your father, is it time to write your own Dear Dad letter?

Chapter 21

Restoring
Family Balance

"Reconciliation and forgiveness are matters of the heart.
They cannot be forced on people."

—GRAEME LEUNG

What is family balance? What do we want it to be? I think we all know when relationships in our families are not going well, but to change them to what we would like is not so easy. In fact, it can be painful, and the road to get there can feel treacherous. I've already described how we get into relational messes and the humility and change of heart required to get back into balance. The chapters on reconciliation help, but often we need practical ideas and guidance to take the necessary steps.

The fact is, this restoration demands such a change of attitude, behavior, thinking, heart, and lifestyle that it requires a hit in the head with a two-by-four, first of all as a wakeup call to the importance of it, second to be willing to face the facts, and third to do what it takes to make changes.

One father I worked with is a great example. I'll call him Todd. Todd was having difficulties relating to his oldest son, Brandon, and with Brandon's worsening behavior. We were able to identify Todd's relationship style as those he learned in his own childhood and copied from his father. It turns out, Todd had related to Brandon the same way he related to everyone else: avoids conflict, avoids setting boundaries, expects others to know what he wants for and from them without telling them, and basically withdraws into his own world wondering why others don't "get it." Todd was soon able to see that Brandon was simply becoming another Todd clone.

By the way, Todd related the same way to his wife, siblings, employees and anyone with whom he had an ongoing relationship. It made life a constant frustration for Todd and everyone else.

That was step one: understanding what was causing this mess in Todd's family. It was a great *aha!* for Todd.

The next step was finding a willingness to make the changes in his own life. At first, it sounded easy. I asked him, "On a scale of one to ten, with ten being high, how important is it to you to make these changes?"

"A ten, of course. I have to do this." Todd was excited. That didn't last long.

I have often used this old riddle, "There were five frogs sitting on a log. Four decided to jump off. How many were left?" The answer is five, because deciding is not the same as doing. Being willing and following through are two very different paradigms. Most of us settle for deciding without doing.

The reality of changing what is so ingrained in the essence of who we are, how we think, and how we behave is no easy step. It takes baby steps, guidance, accountability, and years of hard work based on attitudes of humility, desire, and reconciliation. It's as if all those ways we have always been are addictions that have controlled our very identity. Addictions are a way of hiding.

Todd has made some progress but knows he often takes one step (or more) back for every step forward. This is a lesson for all of us. Just because I say fathers must become involved in the lives of his children, doesn't mean "it's going to be easy so why aren't you doing it?"

Steps in the Right Direction

For that reason, I want to give several methods that may be of help if you are at ten in desire but a one in application.

Find someone to hold you accountable. A wise mentor, counselor, psychotherapist, or life coach will help you understand and walk through the steps. Besides their wisdom of counsel, they have excellent methods and tools of analysis to bring clarity. I guarantee you will not change your ways without accountability.

Learn to "manage from the center." Imagine a continuum. One side is being completely uninvolved, and the other side is being overly involved to the point of controlling. We have seen the damage that uninvolvement does to family relationships, but the overly controlling "my way or the highway" side is also damaging.

We must find balance. In the *center* of the continuum, we find our middle ground. It is from this place that we seek to *help things to go right,* rather than trying to *fix things we see as wrong.*

Whatever we perceive our intention, when we try to fix or correct things we see as wrong, we ignore the input, ideas, values, and "smarts," of others. We ignore their feelings, camaraderie, personal value, and need for a father. Our actions say, "You are wrong, I'm right. You need to change, and I don't." This uncentered attitude invites division rather than solutions. We must value relationships and see others as individuals, not objects to be controlled, directed, and managed.

This concept is presented in a marvelous book called *The Anatomy of Peace.*[1] It has changed the perspective and lifestyle of countless readers, mine included, and I highly recommend it. It shows us that the essence of *helping things to go right* comes from a heart that is outside of the "box," meaning outside of one's limited perspectives, beliefs, biases, and self-centeredness.

Reflect on your own father. The *like father, like son* (or daughter) principle has proved to be one of the most powerful influences I've witnessed in my life. It swiftly provides insight to issues both at home and at work.

That is precisely why I asked Don that fateful question *tell me about your relationship with your father when you were growing up.* I encourage you to answer it now for yourself.

It is amazing the degree to which men and women behave like their fathers, in both good and not so good ways. I have watched fathers and leaders solve systems problems, employee issues, and child dilemmas by examining the childhood relationships they had with their own fathers.

Ask questions. There is an ancient proverb that I use as the basis for my purpose as a coach. It says, "A person's thoughts are like water in a deep well, but someone with insight can draw them out."[2] The coach's job is not to tell someone what to do, but rather to help them discover for themselves who they are and what they want to do. This is best achieved by asking questions.

Asking questions invites openness, vulnerability, and out-of-the-box thinking. It means, "I want to hear what you think, what you want." Remember dads, "A coach's ultimate purpose is helping others to succeed."[3]

If you observe the best interviewers, notice that they will ask a question and after the answer will say, "tell me more," "and then what," and finally they'll just be silent—that's when the best information comes out. We all love to talk about ourselves when we have truly interested listeners who don't have their own agendas. Try this with your kids. Try it with your parents! Google is a great place to find such questions to help you get started.

Practice Appreciative Inquiry (AI). The focus of AI is to identify what is working well and why, and then do more of it. It ignores the urge to fix what might be going wrong. Sound familiar? The difference from Ask Questions above is that it is used with groups rather than one-to-one.

People tend to justify their answers, which is contrary to the inquiry spirit of the AI process. Leadership must make it clear that any answer is acceptable, and its worthiness will be determined as the process evolves. It's also easy to get bogged down by letting the discussion go off track or beyond the group's scope of responsibility. The questions must be solution focused and steer clear of blaming and accusing, narrow-minded thinking, and evoking defensive responses. That might sound like a minefield, but once learned and managed, it gets amazing results for approaching almost any issue at home or at work.

My client, Todd, learned that the way questions are asked and received is paramount. He asked Brandon, "How was school today?" Brandon replied, "It was okay." Big deal. Todd wanted more, so he asked, "If you could change one thing about your day today, what would it be?" "Cancel school," was Brandon's quick answer. Todd was ready: "That's one, give me another." Brandon was thinking now and started telling about an idea. Todd was impressed, "Wow, good idea. What would it take to do that?" "What would be your first step?" "Does that sound like something you really want to do?" Todd was learning to generate "What if" possibility thinking that was building a relationship with his son.

This ability takes planning, confidence, and persistence. Todd's focus was shifting from himself to his son. I'm sure Brandon was wondering, "Who are you and what have you done with my dad?" but he was getting used to it.

Author Stu Weber writes about men as each having four pillars that represent a balanced life and a balanced family. He says, "...the whole family rises to a level of health, fulfillment, and happiness when the King-Warrior-Mentor-Friend (the four pillars) is doing his job and living out God's intention for the masculine soul."[4] Fathers are called to develop people in ways that matter—ways that affect relationships, identity, behavior, values and so on. The father is that ultimate leader, with an awesome ability to lead at home, at work, and in society.

When my client, Todd, reached out to me, he was getting so bogged down from the status quo he couldn't get out of the car when he got home from work. The transition to his current home life was more than he could endure. As he evaluated his role as a husband and father, motivation made him ask, "What do I really want for me, for my wife, for my kids, for my work life, for the future, for today?" It's those questions and answers that drive meaning into life and accountability into making changes that will bring about those answers.

It is easy for dads to get so involved at work that they not only disengage from home but from ideas of purpose and identity. But it is so important. Author Daniel Harkavy has built an impressive program for business owners and managers (and I say for fathers, too) based on this principle. He says:

> We cannot aid you in prioritizing your day or in making decisions with regard to your calendar until we can see what items you believe are most important for your calendar. We cannot determine this until we can see what disciplines and behaviors will allow you to best succeed, as identified in your Business Plan. We cannot assist you with creating a meaningful Business Plan until we understand what you see as the future for your organization and what you see it accomplishing. And we cannot help you to discover and clarify your Business Vision until we can see how your career and company fit into your *overall life*.[5] (emphasis mine)

He has owners work on their Life Plan first. How many of you fathers have spent time developing your Life Plan at all, let alone first? The Life Plan is designed to inform the Vision, Plan, and management of all our priorities— including our daily schedules. It is never too late to start.

In my observation, the young people who have had a father who has been intentional about building identity, values, character, and wise decision making into their lives stand out with maturity, leadership, and wisdom. Their fathers have not left them to figure it out on their own. And most importantly, their fathers have also not left them—neither physically nor passively.

My hope is that Brandon will have this kind of legacy handed down to him as a result of his father's desire to restore family balance.

There is a foundational level of relationship in all of the above methods. By way of review, step one was understanding the father-child relationship and how each one contributes to its success. Step two was deciding to act, to sincerely want to contribute. Step three is to actually follow through, to be proactive about being a father and getting involved.

I've heard many fathers say, "Okay, I want to get more involved, but how? Give me some ideas."

It makes me wonder what keeps men from being so creative at home.

The Three Cs

Each of those methods have at their core three essential elements: commitment, consistency, and communication.

Commitment. This needs to be a deliberate act. The Merriam-Webster Dictionary defines commitment as "The act of giving oneself a charge or trust. An agreement or pledge to do something in the future." As a life coach, when clients agree to action steps that they design for themselves, I always ask, "You know your life and how you live it. What's going to get in the way of you carrying out these steps?" That's a great question to ask your kids. Obstacles for dads include a lack of resources (including but not limited to money), they don't know how, or they're afraid of failing. To that I add one that's not so obvious: the hurt and lack of forgiveness from an unresolved past with their own father. That's a major barrier of which they aren't usually aware.

Consistency. Consistency in a father means being predictable. That includes fulfilling promises made, being available, and being a good role model of behavior, ethics, and values.

A father who is consistent and commits to his role gets to know his children and their mother well enough to know their personalities, friends, likes and dislikes, abilities, quirks, and thoughts. We cannot be present, involved fathers without being committed and consistent.

Communication. Communication is a system for expressing ideas effectively. This means we are able to share and understand each other's thoughts and feelings. This topic generates a great deal of energy from DadsFirst classes because it is so contrary to what tends to be normal for dads.

Dan Crawley lists The 5 Levels of Listening as:[6]

1. Ignoring (especially with preschoolers)

2. Pretend listening (we're preoccupied)

3. Selective listening (when it's something we're interested in)

4. Attentive listening (listening from our own perspective)

5. Empathic listening (listening from the speaker's perspective)

When our youngest son was about four years old, he was talking to his mother who was reading the newspaper. She was only pretending to listen, and he knew it. Finally he reached around the paper, put his hands on either side of her face, and turned it to him. He held it there while he said what he needed to say. He made sure he had her attention.

Dads (and moms), we need to physically demonstrate that we are listening. Make eye contact, get on their level, respond, and restate what they've said. Let them know they matter.

Chapter 22

Finding Our Path Forward

"While it takes two to reconcile, it only takes one to forgive."

—BILL JOHNSON

While working on this book, I read the novel *The Last Librarian* by Brandt Legg and came across this quote by the character Nelson:

"We have to try to find the right path or we become complicit in the crimes against us."

With my heart immersed in this material about fatherlessness, the quote instantly sparked a connection in my mind. And it also raised questions:

- *What are the crimes against us?*
- *How do we become complicit?*
- *Who does "we" refer to?*
- *What is the right path?*

The quote has stayed with me, and I believe it can be usefully applied to a variety of circumstances. But let us consider these questions in the context of fatherlessness.

What are the crimes against us?

These are the results of absent and passive fathers, the fallout of abandoned children that lasts for their lifetime and for generations to come.

These crimes—against our identities, our families, our communities, our nations—were introduced and examined in Parts I and II.

How do we become complicit?

Humans learn by observation and experience—*this is how life is.* We grow up with the pain and disappointment of the father wound, and unless there is an intervention of some kind that changes our experience and understanding, we are assured to pass on that painful wound to those around us and to the next generation. Ignoring and transmitting the wound has become the norm in society, rather than actively seeking solutions.

Who does "we" refer to?

Each one of us has a father. Each one of us has a father wound to some extent, some greater and some lesser. And each one of us passes on the father wound in some way. Each of us has the opportunity to be healed and support healing to those around us.

What is the right path?

The third section of this book provides paths toward reconciliation—the healthiest way to handle and recover from the wound. However, the more I study and get involved in this subject area, the more I am compelled and emotionally invested in what I believe is an ultimate solution and an ultimate father. It is with this conviction that I wrote the Epilogue to come. The stakes are high—it matters.

But what do you when reconciliation seems impossible? Don certainly thought it was.

The Power of the Surrogate Father

"If your father were here right now, what would you want him to say?"

Don sat up straight, his eyes instantly filled with tears, as well as surprise. He blinked a moment and finally stammered out the words, "I love you." He cleared his throat.

"He never said 'I love you.' Nothing I did ever seemed good enough for him. I don't think he liked me. That's why he never said it, why he never showed up."

What is known from empirical research and observation is that the father is designed by role and responsibility to give his children protection, provision, and identity. It is this often-overlooked relationship between a father and his children that is crucial to their well-being and future success. If he is an absent father and no other male father figure is available to give those attributes, his children are, in essence, orphans. This is a tragedy.

According to the online dictionary,[1] the definition of tragedy is *an event causing great suffering, destruction, and distress, such as a serious accident, crime, or natural catastrophe.*

There are events that we don't often name as tragedies but fit the definition: becoming an orphan, being divorced, losing a spouse, or being lost. Each of these falls into the category of being abandoned. Abandonment also includes the tragedy of having an absent uninvolved father.

This was what Don now understood: he had been abandoned.

"Don, as strange as this may sound, with your permission, I'm going to speak to you in the place of your father. I want you to listen to me as if I am your father standing here talking to you. Would that be okay with you?"

His body tensed and his eyes darted as though his dad really was about to show up. It was clear the kinds of negative things Don was used to hearing from him. Nothing any child wants to hear.

"Trust me," I said. "It will be like nothing you've experienced before."

"I guess I can try."

Using Don's own words as a guide, I replied with what the heart of a repentant father might say.

"Don, as your father, I want you to know how sorry I am for not being there for you. I abandoned you when you most needed me. I told myself I was working and gone a lot to provide for you and the family.

"But in reality, I was only thinking about myself. I distanced myself from the consequences through discipline. The fact is, I didn't know how to discipline, or how to be a dad, so instead I chose to be gone. I know you felt that I didn't love you, felt that it was your fault that I was gone. I know it felt like I didn't want to choose you. But none of that is true.

"It was entirely my fault, and I am so sorry. I have wounded you badly. Now that I can see that, all I can say is I love you very much. I *choose* you. Can you ever forgive me?"

By now, we were both in tears. Don stood and dwarfed me with his big bear embrace. It was a powerful moment.

The surrogate father experience is one-sided, but the impact is real. It opens a door the wounded child inside never believed possible. Before Don was able to talk with his father again, before he chose to forgive him, before he wrote his Dead Dad letter (even the raging angry version), the words of love from a surrogate father opened his heart. Even though Don's real father was oblivious at that point and might have never said those words, it didn't matter. Don took his own first step. He opened himself to the prospect of healing his own heart, of being willing to move toward his fallible father, and they began to talk. Before the surrogate father experience, a conversation such as this one had seemed a long way off to Don.

When I first started using the technique of the surrogate father, I couldn't believe that someone would actually accept my words as if coming from their father. But they do, and it makes a life-changing difference every time. Don was able to reach this healing moment without a lot of counseling and time because we didn't try to fix anything—not him or his father or his business. Instead, we went to the crux of the issue: their relationship.

Don realized that he was not at fault for his father abandoning him. Coming to this perspective about his past was necessary to his healing and his future success. He realized that letting go, while still holding his father responsible for what he did or did not do, is important medicine for his father wound. Forgiving our fathers, even when our fathers haven't actually repented, allows the wound we've carried so long to scab over, a temporary relief that leads to eventual healing. This opportunity for healing is open to all who need it.

Accepting Our Imperfection

Humans are imperfect.

Even the best, most engaged and present father will make mistakes. Not only fathers, but every imperfect person we come in contact with, including ourselves. We all carry the power to wound, and even though we may never intend it, wounds will undoubtedly be made.

None of the wounds I received from my father were maliciously given. There was no physical or verbal abuse. This is certainly not true for everyone. Like most, my wound stemmed from my father's blindness: ignorance of his true role, unconscious observation of his father, passivity and anger, and the social norms of the day.

These wounds took root in me when I was a child, when I was most vulnerable and still developing my core identity. It is no surprise that the injury, as well as the recovery, lasted for years, and to some extent remains. But in spite of my wounds, in spite being an imperfect human who has wounded others, I seek to heal and change and make my life and the lives of those around me better.

As I examine my wounds, I better understand why they hurt me so much. And more importantly, I can gradually shift my focus from the father wound inflicted on me as a boy to the wounds I choose to be responsible for as a man. The way I am affected through the pain of abandonment now belongs to me, not him.

I can choose to respond by letting the pain, bitterness, and disappointment remain. Or I can move beyond them, allowing them to be a reminder that my father, like me, was imperfect. I can accept that truth and step into the person I was created to be—one who is free from anger and resentment and able to spread love and forgiveness.

My father passed away several years ago, and each year I see more and more how much I am like him. I still work to end the ways that hinder or harm me and seek to emulate the other ways that are life giving. Because we all have been given both. It is never-ending work, but it is fulfilling nonetheless. I know it would make him proud to see that in me as a reflection of him.

Reconciliation is one of the most powerful forces in the universe. It takes broken pieces and doesn't return them to their previous state, but rather to something greater. Because it is now something that can be shared. The gift of my wound is that I can now find connections with others who have been wounded, and together we can heal and grow.

Embracing Authentic Action

The nation of Ukraine continues to change for the better. While teaching across the country, we heard from leaders in all walks of life that our material on fathering was making a substantial impact. In fact, as I write this in mid-2019, I was just notified that the president of Ukraine finally signed a law establishing an annual national Father's Day. Our organization first introduced that as a bill around 2007.

School administrators were so impacted by our message that one district in Kyiv gave us permission to present our complete seminar to the parents of all the students in their district. There were tens of thousands of students in their district! Unfortunately, it was impossible for us to follow up on their offer due to our lack of personnel—but imagine the potential impact it would have had. Imagine, too, the hunger for this wholesome family structure they were crying out for.

What we have observed in Ukraine is quite simple: Strong fathers result in strong families, which creates strong neighborhoods, schools, and communities, resulting in a strong nation.

The problem of father uninvolvement touches every aspect of our world, in ways we often don't see. Now that you see the connections—the influence and impact—of the role of the father to identity, family, and society at large, you can join the conscious effort to break the cycles that keep us all bound.

Focus on the context of your life and the lives of those around you—the sphere you observe and influence.

> How has the role of the father made an impact on you? On your children?
>
> How has that impact been positive?
>
> How has it been negative?
>
> What identities have been formed?
>
> What wounds are being carried?
>
> What healing needs to take place?
>
> What is your role in that process?
>
> How can you help heal the wounds of father absence and actively support father involvement?
>
> Can you support positive change in your nation? In your state or city?
>
> Can you support it in your community or vocation?
>
> Can you support it in your extended and immediate family?
>
> Can you support it in yourself?

I implore you to seek out the path to healing and take the next right step toward making a difference in someone's life. Especially your own.

"This is not the end of the road; it's the trailhead. What you are journeying toward is freedom, healing, and authenticity."

—JOHN ELDREDGE

Epilogue

The Ultimate Father

"I'll never let you down, never walk off and leave you."

— HEBREWS 13:5 MSG

We all know quite well that humans are imperfect. Every one of us will disappoint and wound others, and every person we meet will fail to live up to our expectations or fully meet our needs at some point. And as natural as it may be for us to develop our identities from our parents, to be influenced by our genetics and our environment, it is not the final word on the subject.

True freedom from our wounds comes when we surrender to a force greater than ourselves. It comes when we realize and accept that this force loves us fully and completely, just as we are. Embracing this love gives us access to everything we need to be whole.

For me, God is this force, the perfect model of love, our Ultimate Father—a father who is always present, always loves and provides. It is in this image of God *who is Love* that I find my true identity, one that cannot be tainted by the wounds of this world. The Gospel of the Bible is a love story from our Ultimate Father to us, His children, and an invitation into a relationship with Him.

The Gospel shows us how to love by seeing ourselves and others not through humanity's eyes but through the eyes of our Ultimate Loving Father.

Knowing who we are and how we're wired, God implies specific guidance to earthly fathers, "You are to represent me to your family and the world." If only our earthly fathers loved with the presence and steadfastness of our Heavenly Father! But even in our ever-present imperfection, surrendering to the love of our Creator and modeling that love to others, we can not only live well ourselves, but also faithfully pass on this liberating wisdom and truth to the next generation.

It is with perspective that DadsFirst uses the last verses of the Old Testament as the foundation for its fathering ministry:

> Behold, I will send you Elijah the prophet [a reference to John the Baptist] before the coming of the great and dreadful day of the Lord. And he will turn the hearts of the fathers to the children, and the hearts of the children to their fathers, lest I come and strike the earth with a curse.[1]

I believe the curse referred to here is the father wound and applies to all of us. Gordon Dalbey underscores this by saying, "It implies that the brokenness in this world between children and fathers reflects the brokenness between humanity and God."[2] Just imagine, the entire Old Testament ends with words about the broken relationship between fathers and their children.

This separation from the Ultimate Father began in the garden of Eden and has continued ever since. It is reflected in our separation from our earthly fathers. More than anything, the world needs reconciliation between fathers and their children, but in order to do that, the ultimate solution is reconciliation between each one of us and our Heavenly Father. And it is for this precise purpose that Jesus came: to restore that relationship between our Creator and all of humanity.

I have presented many scenarios about the absent father dilemma with problems and solutions, but as I see it, the answers are found in a relationship with the Ultimate Father of us all. He is personified as the Hound of Heaven[3] and will never stop pursuing each one of us to come to know

Him in this relationship. That's the way I believe we were designed and the way the relationship works best.

Author Malcolm Gladwell said, "Successes in the life of a father and son are not accidents or random occurrences, they arise out of a predictable and powerful set of circumstances, forces, and opportunities."[4]

My belief is that Gladwell is right; they are not accidents, but are part of the plan of a loving, ultimate father: God. We have gotten so used to living without Him that feeling abandoned is the new normal. This is the curse: that we would believe that this broken world of broken relationships is all there is and all we are meant to have.

But we have access to true healing, identity, and fulfillment through the love of our Creator.

How important is this to our Ultimate Father?

"For God so loved the world that he gave his one and only Son, that whoever believes in him shall not perish but have eternal life."[5]

Imagine—life forever with your Father, who loves you very much!

Appendix

Dear Dad:

How are you doing on this [crossed out] fine day. I trust that all is well and that you're having a pleasant day..... I have five questions.. who did you abandon me for? when did you abandon me? why did you abandon me? what was more important than me, your son? where did you go??

If you were my son, nothing in this world would have [crossed out] caused me to abandon you. I would have loved you and cared for you like I love and care for myself..... No matter how you try to ignore the fact that you have a son, your soul will never allow you to forget about your own flesh and blood. I'm not upset at you for your short commings* Dav 5:16

*I honor you because my father above you told me to love instead of hate.

Willie [redacted]

Age: 33

7

Dear Dad:

I like to say that even if you are no here with me now, I wish you spend time with me when I was a little boy, and talking about that I wasn't agree that way you treat my brothers and my mother.

Any way you was my father, and I love you and I never talkyou that, because you never spend time with me alone.

Dad I love you but in the same time I was afraid of you, because of you way you treat us

Some time I wish to have a hut and a kiss from you, and few work that Love me

Any way. I forgiveyou
and I love you

Marco ████ 41

Jeff ▓▓▓▓ Age 45

Dear Dad:

I Just wanted to tell you that I love you and that I understand. How hard your life must have been. I know you really tried to be there for your family but work had to come into the picture. I know life with Ma and you fighting and arguing all the time was very bad for the whole family. I know we had a lot of good times mixed with the bad times and sometimes it is hard to Seperate the two. Growing up in that crazy mess, now that I look back at it it was crazy. It has been hard for me to get it right in my mind what a good marriage and family is really. I am thankful for some of the times that we spent as I became a adult but some of me never quite fully grew up I am still working on that. I am glad that I was able to see you Still caring for Ma in the end when She was dieing that last year must have been the hardest part of your life. That taught me a lot about not giving up on people even those that hurt you. I just wanted to tell you that you are very special to me and I forgive you for your failings as a father I realize you did your very best you knew how. I pray the Lord will work in your life to give you the peace of Jesus Christ that He has given me.

Love Jeff

Dear Dad:

40 yrs.

Bryan ████

You have no Idea what **Not** having a father around has done in my life. No principles, no Discipline no Encouragement from a stable father figure, so I learn from the world what a father should be and I have done to my own son what you have done to me. But because of this God has been my father, and now I have to learn 30+ yrs of what I could of been. You never pursued me, why?, you could of at least tried, But you Did not. For a long time I need you, wondered about you, because of this I hardly know who I really am except what God says about me. I plan on breaking this cycle with my son what you did to me.

I ask god to give me the strength to forgive you and to **NOT** do to my son what you have done to me.

Goodbye.

Father Hunger

Page 3

214 | Tim Olson

Endnotes

Chapter 2—The Story of Ukraine

1. Askold Krushelnycky, "Ukraine Famine," Ukrainian Archives and News, 2003. http://www.faminegenocide.com/resources/ukraine_famine.html.

2. Organization for Economic Co-operation and Development (36 member OECD countries) http://www.oecd.org/els/soc/SF_1_2_Children_in_families.pdf.

3. Terry Wolfgram, "Engaging Fathers," presented at Healthy Families—Green Bay. Accessed online, July 2019, http://studylib.net/doc/5514771/wolfgramengaging-fathers.

Chapter 3—Defining Father Presence and Absence

1. Google Dictionary Authorized By Oxford Press, https://en.wikipedia.org/wiki/Google_Dictionary.

2. Ibid, Google Dictionary

3. US Census Bureau data representing children under age 18 living without a biological, step, or adoptive father. Population Reference Bureau Census 2017, American Community Survey. https://www.census.gov/data/tables/time-series/demo/families/children.html.

4. Ibid, Population Reference Bureau Census 2017,

5. Ibid, Terry Wolfgram

6. Ibid, Organization for Economic Co-operation and Development (36 member OECD countries).

7. Even though the US Census Bureau is always cited as the source, these figures can have many interpretations and appear differently depending on who is doing the reporting and interpreting.

8. Ibid, Terry Wolfgram

Chapter 4—Recognizing Father Absence

1.   Andrew Miller, *Absentee Fathers Are Destroying the United States,* "The Extent of Fatherlessness," February 2018 https://www.thetrumpet. com/16885-absentee-fathers-are-destroying-the-united-states.

2.   "Suicide," *Psychology Today.* Accessed online, July 2019. https://www. psychologytoday.com/basics/suicide.

3.   This is a description I personally heard VanVonderen use several times in in-person presentations.

4.   I believe each one of us is unique in terms of our character qualities, personality traits, gifting, skills, and abilities. Everyone wants to know who they are and what their purpose is. It is a part of our identity. Our significant goal in life is to discover how that uniqueness combines and works out as the "person we were meant to be."

Chapter 5—A Father's Impact

1.   J. H. Pleck and Masciadrelli, B. P., "Paternal Involvement by U.S. Residential Fathers: Levels, Sources, and Consequences," in M. E. Lamb (Ed.), *The role of the father in child development* (Hoboken, NJ, US: John Wiley & Sons Inc., 2004) pp. 222-271.

2.   B.J. Zvara, Sarah J. Schoppe-Sullivan, and Claire M. Kamp Dush, "Fathers' Involvement in Child Health Care: Associations with Prenatal Involvement, Parents' Beliefs, and Maternal Gatekeeping," Published online, Aug 24, 2013

3.   Nicole Letourneau and Gerald Giesbrecht, "Even When Baby's in the Womb, Dads Have an Influence," Updated 06/16/2017, https://www.huffingtonpost.ca/nicole-letourneau/fathers-and-baby-development_b_5473964.html.

4.   "CFRP Policy Brief | B.020.0914," Child and Family Research Partnership, Published online, September 2014.

5.   W.L. Coleman, Garfield, C.F., and the Committee on Psychosocial Aspects of Child and Family Health. "Fathers and Pediatricians: Enhancing Men's Roles in the Care and Development of their Children," American Academy of Pediatrics Policy Statement, Pediatrics, May, 2004.

6.   Ibid W.L. Coleman.

7.   Kendra Cherry, "Trust vs. Mistrust: Psychosocial Stage 1, Learning to trust the world around us," Updated July 16, 2019. https://www.verywellmind.com/trust-versus-mistrust-2795741.

8.   Anna Sutherland, "Family Structure and Children's Health," Institute for Family Health. Accessed online, July 2019. https://ifstudies.org/blog/family-structure-and-childrens-health/.

9.   Gayatri Pagdi, "The father-son relationship," Complete Wellbeing, February 2007. https://completewellbeing.com/article/his-fathers-son/

10.   Bisi Adewale, "Parental Involvement And Children's Well-being," August 2016. https://bisiadewale.com/2016/08/parental-involvement-and-childrens-well-being

11.   Michaela B. Upshaw,Cheryl R. Kaiser and Jessica A. Sommerville, "Parents' empathic perspective taking and altruistic behavior predicts infants' arousal to others' emotions," *Frontiers in Psychology*, Published online April 2015.

12.   "Father Involvement in Early Childhood Programs," Minnesota Fathers, 2013. http://www.mnfathers.org/wp-content/uploads/2013/06/Early-Childhood-Sector-Analysis.pdf.

13.   Ibid J.H. Pleck

14.   Ibid Minnesota Fathers

15.   "Performance Improvement 2009. How does involvement of nonresident fathers affect what happens to their children in foster care?" Office of the Assistant Secretary for Planning and Evaluation, January 2009. https://aspe.hhs.gov/report/performance-improvement-2009/how-does-involvement-nonresident-fathers-affect-what-happens-their-children-foster-care.

16.   "Responsible Fatherhood Toolkit: Resources from the Field," National Responsible Fatherhood Clearinghouse. Accessed online, July 2019. https://www.fatherhood.gov/toolkit/work/child-welfare.

17.   "More about the Dads: Exploring Associations between Nonresident Father Involvement and Child Welfare Case Outcomes," Department of Health and Human Services. Accessed online, July 2019. http://site.americanhumane.org/fatherhooddocs/intro_handouts.pdf.

18.   Edward Kruk PhD, "Father Absence, Father Deficit, Father Hunger," Psychology Today, May 2012. https://www.psychologytoday.com/us/blog/co-parenting-after-divorce/201205/father-absence-father-deficit-father-hunger.

19.   Ibid Edward Kruk

20.   Ibid Edward Kruk

21.   Sarah Klein, "8 Reasons to Make Time for Family Dinner," Health, March 2016. https://www.health.com/health/gallery/0,,20339151,00.html?slide=125106#125106.

22.   Ibid Edward Kruk

23.   "The Consequences of Fatherlessness," Fathers.com. Accessed online, July 2019. http://fathers.com/statistics-and-research/the-consequences-of-fatherlessness/.

24.   Sheala Catherine Morrison, "The Presentation of Childhood Parental Divorce in Adulthood: A Retrospective Phenomenological Study," Presented December 2014, University of Nevada, Las Vegas. With permission, morris14@unlv.nevada.edu

25.   Traci Pedersen, "Parents' Incarceration Can Have Long-Lasting Impact on Kids' Health," Psych Central. Updated July 2018. https://psychcentral.com/news/2018/07/18/parents-incarceration-can-have-long-lasting-impact-on-kids-health/137070.html.

26.   Gabriella Kortsch, "Fatherless Women: What Happens to the Adult Woman who was Raised Without her Father?" Accessed online, July 2019. https://trans4mind.com/counterpoint/index-happiness-wellbeing/kortsch4.html.

27.   Ben Spencer, "Growing up without a father can permanently alter the BRAIN: Fatherless children are more likely to grow up angry and turn to drugs," *DailyMail*, December 2013. https://www.dailymail.co.uk/sciencetech/article-2518247/Growing-father-permanently-alter-BRAIN-Fatherless-children-likely-grow-angry-turn-drugs.html.

28.   Amy Guertin, "The Effect on Men That Grow Up Without a Father Figure," Our Everyday Life. Accessed online, July 2019. https://oureverydaylife.com/effect-men-grow-up-father-figure-43045.html.

29.   Anne Reed, "DNA Evidence: Effects of Fatherlessness," American Family Radio, August 2017. https://www.afa.net/the-stand/family/2017/08/dna-evidence-effects-of-fatherlessness/#.WaLiYMSpHQZ.facebook.

30.   Ibid Edward Kruk PhD

Chapter 6—The Active Choice of Presence

1.   The Dear Dad letter is introduced in the second lesson of the DadsFirst 10 lesson series, Father Hunger. The lesson describes how powerful and impact the father has in one's life whether for good or bad, and the letter makes it personal. It may be the hardest letter they ever write and may be written through anger, bitterness, gratitude, sorrow, or guilt. Its purpose is to help see the impact of one's own father, to accept him and resolve to not repeat his mistakes and to continue those things he did well in his fathering. Although often begun with rage and blame, it is not written to blame but to understand. Writers are encouraged to express their thoughts and feelings they may have never shared with their dads or even considered themselves.

The letter may need a few attempts, and in fact, a second letter is encouraged several lessons later after deeper understanding is achieved in further lessons. It may help to restore the relationship but at the very least is a healing balm for the writer. Four actual letters from class members are included in the Appendix.

2.   K. Malm, Murray J. and Geen R. "What About the Dads? Child Welfare Agencies' Efforts to Identify, Locate and Involve Nonresident Fathers," US Department of Health and Human Services, Office of the Assistant Secretary for Planning and Evaluation, 2006.

3.   Current Population Survey Annual Social and Economic Supplement, US Census Bureau and US Bureau of Labor Statistics.

4.   Stu Weber, *Four Pillars of a Man's Heart: Bringing Strength Into Balance*, (Colorado Springs, CO, US: Multnomah Books, a division of Random House, Inc., 1997) p. 28.

5. Ibid Stu Weber

Chapter 7—Origins of Identity

1. I.A. Khan, "Is identity given to us or do we create our own?"2007. Accessed online http://www.markedbyteachers.com/gcse/sociology/is-identity-given-to-us-or-do-we-create-our-own.html.

2. J. Oberuč and Zapletal, L "Family as One of the Most Important Factors in a Child's Upbringing," *Acta Educationis Generalis* volume 7, 2017, issue 2.

3. B. Gaultiere, "Shaping Your Child's Image of God." Accessed online, July 2019. https://www.soulshepherding.org/shaping-your-childs-image-of-god/.

4. Ibid Oberuč and Zalletal

5. John Eldredge, *Wild at Heart: Discovering the Secret of a Man's Heart*, (Thomas Nelson Publishers, Nashville, 2001), p. 28.

6. Dr. M. Meeker, "Why Daughters Need their Dads," 2016. Accessed online, http://blog.lifeway.com/leadingmen/2016/01/05/why-daughters-need-their-dads/#. WhXC8kqnGUk.

7. J. Toussaint, (Cited by Katie FitzGerald, Director of Communications at Walden Behavioral Care), "How Dads Can Help Foster Positive Body Image In Their Daughters." Accessed online, July 2019. https://www.waldeneatingdisorders. com/a-dads-influence-on-his-daughters-body-image,/

8. Dr M. Rapini, "Studies Show Dads Give Girls Most Of Their Self-Esteem Before Age 12," National Parents Organization. Accessed online, July 2019. https:// nationalparentsorganization.org/blog/3924-psychotherapist-st-3924.

9. Ibid John Eldridge

Chapter 8—The Father Wound

1. Roland Warren, https://www.faithgateway.com/bad-dads-holes-wounded-souls.

2. Ibid Roland Warren

3. Gordon Dalbey, "Healing the Father Wound," 1997, http://www.abbafather.com/ articles/article_hfw.pdf

4. Dan B. Allender, PhD, *To Be Told: God Invites You to Coauthor Your Future,* (Colorado Springs, Waterbrook Press, a Division of Random House, Inc., 2005), p.77.

5. Bill Moyers, "A Gathering of Men," Public Affairs Television, 1990. https://www-tc. pbs.org/moyers/journal/archives/gatheringofmen.pdf.

6. Ibid Gordon Dalbey

7.   Randy Hix, *The Affirmation Crisis*, (Elm Hill Brooks, Nashville, 2018), p. 39.

8.   Ibid Dan Allender.

9.   Quenching the Father Thirst, National Center for Fatherhood, http://fathers.com/wp-content/uploads/2019/03/Quenching-the-Father-Thirst-Curriculum-Overview.pdf

10.   Ibid John Eldredge.

11.   Amanda Vogt, "Gangs a Cry for Family?" Chicago Tribune, 1996. https://www.chicagotribune.com/news/ct-xpm-1996-12-24-9612240065-story.html.

12.   Ibid Amanda Vogt

13.   Ibid Stu Weber, p. 28

14.   See Negative Agreements, chapter 14

Chapter 9—The Father Influence in Action

1.   The Arbinger Institute, *Leadership and Self-Deception:Getting Out of the Box,* (Berrett-Hoehler Publishers, Inc., San Francisco, 2010), p. 7

2.   Ibid., p.140

3.   For a thorough presentation of this critical topic, I urge the reader to read Leadership and Self-Deception by the Arbinger Institute. You will understand why it has been translated into twenty languages and is required reading prior to being hired at many businesses. Take a moment to consider all those around you in terms of how you see them and how you see yourself in relationship to them.

4.   Richard Rohr, *Adam's Return: The Five Promises of Male Initiation*, (The Crossroad Publishing Company, New Youk, 2004), p. 111

5.   Shaquille O'Neal, "Biological Didn't Bother," Listen online, https://www.youtube.com/watch?v=y2J5xEOIoCA.

Chapter 10—Fathers out of Balance

1.   Jeff VanVonderen, *Tired of Trying to Measure Up: Getting free from the demands, expectations, and intimidations of well-meaning people*, (Bethany House Publishers, Minneapolis, 1989), pp. 33-38

2.   Ibid, p.36

Chapter 11—Families out of Balance

1.   Dr. Susan Forward and Torres, Joan, *Men Who Hate Women and the Women Who Love Them: When Loving Hurts and You Don't Know*, (A Bantam Book, New York, 1986), pp. 99-125

2.   Joanna Nicola, "Disarming Defense Mechanisms Triggered by Shame," The Nicola Method. Accessed online, July 2019. http://www.nicolamethodforhighconflict.com/defense-mechanisms-triggered-by-shame/.

3.   Jung, C.G., "Shame is a Soul-Eating Emotion," Published online, 2018. https://carljungdepthpsychologysite.blog/2018/10/21/shame-is-a-soul-eating-emotion-carl-jung/#.XTnO9PZFyUk.

4.   Marilyn Sorensen, *Breaking the Chain of Low Self-Esteem*, 2nd Ed., (Wolf Publishing, Sherwood, OR 2006).

Chapter 12—Businesses out of Balance

1.   John L. Ward, *Perpetuating the Family Business: 50 Lessons learned from Long-Lasting, Successful Families In Business*, (Pagrave MacMillan, New York, NY, 2004), p. 503

2.   T. Stoltzfus, "Support Structures in the Coaching Relationship," Published online, 2012. http://www.christiancoachingcenter.org/index.php/2012/01/support-structures-in-the-coaching-relationship-by-tony-stoltzfus-9/. [used with permission.]

Chapter 13—When the Past Invades the Present

1.   Ben Dattner, PhD, "Re-enacting family dynamics in the workplace," Psychology Today, 2011. https://www.psychologytoday.com/us/blog/credit-and-blame-work/201104/re-enacting-family-dynamics-in-the-workplace.

Chapter 14—The Truth about Transference

1.   Richard Rohr and Feister, John, *Things Hidden: Scripture as Spirituality*, (Cincinnati, St. Anthony Messenger Press, 2008).,

Chapter 15—The Path of Anger

1.   The American Heritage® Dictionary of the English Language, 5th Edition, viewed at https://www.wordnik.com/words/anger.

2.   Henryk, Wieja, MD, "Spiritual Fatherhood," January 2015. https://www.youtube.com/watch?v=F3r_7McyENQ.

3.   Ibid Henryk, Wieja, MD

4.   Paul F. Singh, MA LP, *Rekindling Your Spirit: A Spiritual Journey into Personal Change Intimacy and Sexuality*, (Lantern Publishing, 2006), p. 43. [used with permission]

5.   Jay Borgard, *Pissed*, 2014. Research project, accessed online, July 2019. https://vimeo.com/80901057.

6.   Julian Melgosa, PhD, *Anger Management: Anger Control Strategies From a Christian Perspective*, Presentation slide #19. Accessed online, July 2019. https://slideplayer.com/slide/4600617/.

7.   Ibid Rohr, *Adam's Return*, p. 37

8.   Ibid Rohr, *Adam's Return*

Chapter 16—A Visit to the Halfway House

1.   See examples in the Appendix

Chapter 17—When Anger Spreads to Society

1.   Ibid Paul F. Singh

2.   Harassment, https://www.eeoc.gov/laws/types/sexual-harassment.cfm

Chapter 18—Addressing Our Roots

1.   Pace University, "Stalin's Oxymorons: Social State, Law and Family." Accessed online, July 2019. http://webpage.pace.edu/nreagin/tempmotherhood/spring02i/Stalin/historicalpage.html#top.

2.   Joshua Rubenstein, "Stalin's Children," *New York Times,* November 25, 2007.

3.   You can find more information about their activities and compelling vision and mission on their website: www.icfatherhood.org.

Chapter 19—The Power of Reconciliation

1.   Ibid Richard Rohr, *Things Hidden*

2.   Corinthians 5:18 (MSG)

3.   Matt 3:16

Chapter 20—Reconciliation in Individuals

1. Arthur A. Rouner, Jr., *Forgiveness: The Road to Reconciliation*, (Writers Press, an imprint of iUniversal, Inc., 2002), p. 42.

2. Ken Canfield, *The Heart of a Father*, (Chicgo, Northfield Publishing, 1996) p. 54

Chapter 21—Restoring Family Balance

1. The Arbinger Institute, *The Anatomy of Peace,* (San Francisco, Berrett-Koehler Publishers, Inc., 2007), p. 203.

2. Proverbs 20:5 (GNV)

3. Daniel Harkavy, *Becoming A Coaching Leader: The Proven Strategy for Building Your Own Team of Champions*, (Nashville, Thomas Nelson Publishers, 2007), p.34.

4. Ibid Stu Weber

5. Ibid Daniel Harkavy

6. Dan Crawley, "The Five Levels of Listening (How To Be a Better Listener)," March 2013, https://www.doncrawley.com/the-five-levels-of-listening-how-to-be-a-better-listener/

Chapter 22— Finding Our Path Forward

1. Google Dictionary Authorized By Oxford Press, https://en.wikipedia.org/wiki/Google_Dictionary.

Epilogue

1. Malachi 4:5-6 (KJV)

2. Ibid Gordon Dalbey

3. Francis Thompson, "The Hound of Heaven."

4. Malcolm Gladwell, *Outliers: The Story of Success* (New York, Little, Brown and Company, 2008), p. 155.

5. John 3:16 (WEB)

Acknowledgements

While I always did a lot of writing, I never thought I could write a book. In looking back, there were life-shaping people who have contributed to the process and for whom I am grateful.

To my mom, who had dementia to the point she often didn't know who I was. When I told her I was writing a book I paused a few moments not expecting a response. But then she floored me by saying, "So, do you want to talk about it?" Thanks, Mom, for waking up to that brief moment of encouragement.

To my dad, for finally being comfortable in your 80s telling us you love us.

To my wife, Kay, for your patience. You will finally have your husband back.

To Chuck Aycock, Executive Director of the National Fathering Ministry (DadsFirst) for your vast heart, experience, and understanding of absent and uninvolved fathers.

To Kimberly Kessler, my insightful and selfless editor without whom my book would be really bad. You are an exceptional editor.

To the Open Door Writers Group. You never ceased to amaze me with your insights into how to improve my writing. Thank you.

To the young fathers at Wildwood Church in the 1970s who unwittingly mentored and modeled fatherhood and manhood to me as a young man You were the intervention I needed to move from the passive influence of my own father to become the father, husband, and role model I was always intended to be.

About the Author

Tim Olson is an author, educator, pastor, and life coach. His understanding of father-child relationships was fostered through years of observation and application in education, coaching clients around the world, and working with the National Fathering Ministry in Minnesota and Ukraine. Through it all, he's found his way to helping others to discover who they are meant to be and then walking with them to maximize their discovery. Tim and his wife, Kay, have been married for 53 years and are blessed with three children, six grandchildren, four bonus grandchildren, and four great grandchildren.